SINGING PRAISES

Annie McDonnell has long been a respected member of the literary community as a professional book reviewer, but many of her colleagues didn't know that she was also an essayist and poet—until now.

"If you want to see what a heart looks like, broken into words, read this book. If you want to see what courage looks like, brick by brick all the way to heaven…read this book."

—**Jeff Arch**, author of award-winning novel *"Attachments"* and Oscar nominee for *"Sleepless in Seattle"*

"'Annie's Song' is an open-hearted memoir about a life spent loving the most vulnerable among us. These are stories full of joy and life that keep loved ones close, even after they've passed from this world. This poetic writing of untiring advocacy, compassionate witness, and deep love is a gift to the enormous community of writers— yes, those who have felt seen and uplifted by Annie McDonnell over the years, but also those who might be hearing her voice saying 'you matter' for the first time. This book is our chance to see how a life of empathy is born."

—**Diane Zinna**, author of *"The All-Night Sun"*

"A true, honest, powerful voice, and she puts it to beautiful use in 'Annie's Song.' And she's right: The prose sings."

—**Darin Strauss**, author of *"The Queen of Tuesday"*

"A fresh and welcome voice in literature."

—**Camille Pagán**, the bestselling author of *"Good for You"*

"While some confronted with challenging life circumstances would be ground down, McDonnell has used her experiences with miscarriage, grief, and illness to hone herself into a fine diamond. This book is a tale of loss, but it also shimmers with the joy of discovering one's true self amidst the chaos."

—**Tonya Mitchell**, author of *"A Feigned Madness"*

"Whether it's lost children, lost friends, or a body slowly breaking down, Annie McDonnell reveals both the joy and heartbreak in a life spent carrying 'luggage I could never unpack.'"

—**Marco Rafalà**, author of *"How Fires End,"*
winner of the Italian American Association Book Award

"...innovative and insightful. A very cool way to talk about our life. We need more creative memoirs like it."

—**Piper Huguley**, author of *"By Her Own Design"*

"Few people have done more for readers and writers than Annie McDonnell. Annie's latest contribution is her long anticipated literary work. The essays and poems take the reader on Annie's unparalleled journey of fierce love and tragic losses. The words beautifully tear at your heart and lift you up daring you, too, to face hard challenges and still find joy."

—**Grace Sammon**, author of *"The Eves"* and host of *"The Storytellers"*

"This memoir of a woman facing her own passing speaks of love in its many iterations and of the strength that love brings into her life. With a strong voice and forgiving heart, McDonnell writes tenderly of unconditional 'puppy love' and powerfully of missing the love of a lost child. Though crippled with a debilitating illness, McDonnell rises above and grabs the reader by the heart with a moving testament to the human spirit."

—**Dawn Reno Langley**, author of more than 30 books

"An honest, emotional, heartfelt, memorable, and thought-provoking book that will touch your soul."

—**Linda Zagon**, *"Linda's Book Obsession,"* book reviewer, and influencer

"Annie McDonnell may have a frail body, but she has the heart of a lion and the mind of a poet. With prose and poems both heartbreaking and uplifting, she has painted poignant and beautiful word pictures that invite readers into a world filled with both physical pain and boundless love for the humans and fur babies in her life. Carefully selected popular songs are the perfect companions for all her works, especially my favorite, 'Move Me.'"

—**Mickey Goodman**, author/ghostwriter of memoirs and journalist

"A powerful mixed genre memoir, 'Annie's Song', is, as the author herself says, 'a love song to trauma survivors, dog lovers, people who make wishes, love seekers, and dreamers.' But it's also a tribute to Annie's perseverance in the face of incredible suffering. Her beautiful poetry and lyrical prose are full of heartfelt pain, but also hope."

—**Susan Cushman**, author of eight books, including
the mixed genre memoir *"Pilgrim Interrupted"*

"This is a stirring memoir constructed with tears and laughter, bonded together with joy and slices of pain."

—**Eoin Dempsey**, bestselling author of *"White Rose,"*
"Black Forest," and *"The Longest Echo"*

"Filled with wisdom, sorrow and healing these essays and poems are borne from great loss, the weight of illness, and love. Annie McDonnell shares her dreams, her fears and her deeply felt emotions with candor and courage. Fall into 'Annie's Song' to feel the weight of the human experience."

—**Carol Van Den Hende**, award-winning author of
"Orchid Blooming" and *"Goodbye, Orchid"*

"...brims full with ache, loss, and above all, big-hearted love. Not to be missed!

—**Jennifer Rosner**, award winning author of
"The Yellow Bird Sings" and *"Once We Were Home"*

"It was a deeply moving experience to sit with Annie's words and images of love and loss and longing. By giving so completely of herself, Annie brought me to tears of recognition of all the beauty—and its opposite—in my own life. I recommend 'Annie's Song' as a wonderful exploration of the deepest—and often most hidden—parts of all of us."

—**Deborah Goodrich Royce**, award-winning author of
"Reef Road," "Ruby Falls," and *Finding Mrs. Ford"*

"Annie McDonnell, creator of *The Write Review*, is an insightful interviewer who has been an avid advocate for writers and readers since 2006. In her heartfelt memoir, she shares the experiences that have transformed her, showing how loved ones can lift us up with their kindness or destroy us with their callousness. Her story will win your heart."

—**Janet Skeslian Charles**, *New York Times* bestselling author
"The Paris Library"

"Annie McDonnell has devoted years to bringing other authors' voices to the world. Now she is sharing her own words... open, honest, raw, and poignant."

—**Patricia Sands**, author of the "Love in Provence" Series and more

"This is a book I highly recommend for folks who are struggling with loss. Whether it is the loss of your own life and wellbeing or the loss of someone you love, this book will help you understand the losses you faced in a different light."

—**Phyllis Jones Pisanelli**, book reviewer and blogger

"Wow! 'Annie's Song' grabs hold of your heart in the very beginning and does not let go. A raw and highly emotional look inside the heart of a woman with everything to lose and nothing to gain. At times inspiring and uplifting, and at times heartbreaking, this powerful story will stay with you long after you have turned the last page. Highly recommended."

—**Bette Lee Crosby**, *USA Today* bestselling author

"...filled with raw emotion that will at times bring you to tears. The beautiful prose floats off the page, and the pain and longing in her essays and poems is striking. McDonnell has a powerful way of bringing the reader in to her world. A must read for anyone who has ever experienced the hard things in life, which is most of us."

—**Leslie A. Rasmussen**, award-winning author of
"After Happily Ever After" and *"The Stories We Cannot Tell"*

"A treat for the senses and a journey of the heart that will ultimately touch your soul. A must read!"

—**Meg Nocero**, award-winning author of
"The Magical Guide to Bliss, Sparkle & Shine" and
"Butterfly Awakens: A Memoir of Transformation through Grief"

"Lyrical and heartfelt, Annie's Song hits all the right notes–exploring subjects like love, loss and the trial and tribulations we face in life with an honest lens. Breathtakingly honest, heartwarming, and poignant."

—**Samantha Vérant**, author of *"Seven Letters from Paris"*

"Annie writes with such sincere passion that I felt like I was experiencing these things with her and could feel the emotion and joy in each and every essay. Anyone that has ever had difficulty pushing through difficult stages of their life should read this book for heartfelt inspiration and to gain the ability to see past the obstacles that are placed in one's path and find the light at the end, no matter how dim it may seem at times."

—**Serena Soape**, avid reader, book reviewer, book influencer and began The Write Review Book Club with Annie

"An inspiring true story of one woman's battle against a rare and debilitating neurological illness, Stiff Person Syndrome. The book is beautifully written and told with unflinching honesty. Annie's story is uplifting, poignant and a gift that will give readers greater empathy for loved ones struggling with chronic illness.

—**Susan Schild**, *USA Today* bestselling author

"Annie opens her heart and invites us in. She had me at hello."

—**Vince Spinnato**, memoir *"My Pursuit of Beauty: A Cosmetic Chemist Reveals the Glitz, the Glam, and the Batsh*t Crazy,"* biographical documentary *"Skin Deep,"* and founder of VS Vincenzo Ltd., Inc.

"A brave and moving portrait of one woman's struggle to survive in the face of great physical challenges and lack of emotional support. The author has spilled her great big heart onto every page. If resiliency was a life test, McDonnell could lead the class!"

—**Suzanne Simonetti**, *USA Today* bestselling author of *"The Sound of Wings"*

"A deeply personal, emotional and incredibly moving collection of essays and poems that will stay with me long after turning the final page."

—**Soraya M. Lane**, bestselling author of *The London Girls*

"A tireless advocate for aspiring writers (including myself), Annie McDonnell's debut memoir offers an unflinching glimpse into her beautiful soul and tragic past. While the view is often dark, glimmers of light persistently shine through, and we are reminded that loss and grief—while indelible—need not define us."

—**Frank M. Oliva**, author of *"Walking Among the Trees"*

"A slice of resilience and kindness in an unfair world. A reminder that love is all that really matters."

—**Mary Turner Thomson**, international bestselling author

"An intimate glimpse into an extraordinary life, written with immense compassion, humanity, and heart."

—**Eddy Boudel Tan**, award winning author of
"After Elias" and *"The Rebellious Tide"*

"Poignant, heart-wrenching, riveting, and beautifully-written, a must-read for 2023. I loved this unforgettable book so much!"

—**May Cobb**, award-winning author of
"My Summer Darlings" and *"The Hunting Wives"*

"Her writing is transformational, taking the reader to a place of understanding, connection, and love.

—**Lauri Schoenfeld**, author of *Little Owl*

"An inviting and transcendent mixture of poetry and prose, Annie's Song welcomes us deeply into the bright soul of a champion of stories and storytellers. With candor and grace, Annie McDonnell chronicles heartrending loss and trauma, but also those illuminating, essential moments of unimaginable empathy, compassion, and perseverance which teach us what a life well-lived and well-loved can and must be."

—**Jonathan Haupt**, coeditor,
"Our Prince of Scribes: Writers Remember Pat Conroy"
and Executive Director of the Pat Conroy Literary Center

"Picture a warm sunny day with a soft breeze and white clouds in the sky. As you lie in the grass and close your eyes, Annie transports you to her vivid world filled with love and heartbreak, health and illness, joy, and sorrow. By sharing her creative fiction memoir, like a dandelion shares its seed in the wind, she allows the reader to explore a gamut of emotions, some welcome and some uncomfortable, but all thought provoking and powerful. Annie has survived multiple traumatic experiences such as the murder of her best friend, a devastating car crash, and the diagnosis of an incurable chronic illness. Having met Annie in college, I have witnessed her rebuild herself again and again through the written word and now she is sharing those uninhibited moments in this book. Her poetic debut is not to be missed and you may find yourself reading it over and over to fully capture and digest her incredible journey. Highly recommend!"

—**Erica Firkin**, avid reader and book reviewer

"'Because I have ...a story to tell.' With these poetic words–more a gentle cry–we see the author's song, a whisper of love, both striking and revelatory. At times heartbreaking, at other times, one of the most productive creative forces for body and soul 'Annie's Song' is an incantation of emotion and truth."

–**Diana Paul**, author of *"Things Unsaid"*

"A rich, multi-faceted, and multi-genre view of one life that shows all of us the power of endurance, understanding, and perseverance. There's something here for everyone, and the reader will come away richly rewarded."

—**David Bell**, *New York Times* bestselling author of
"She's Gone" and *"Try Not to Breathe"*

"Annie takes you on an emotional journey with her expansive prose. This is writing for real life that sticks with you and changes your perspective. It does what a book is supposed to do with elegance and excellent pacing."

–**Jade & Wilnona**, The And I Thought Ladies

"...details what we do when our world falls apart in the ways we least expect. It is about resilience and deep despair. Annie shows us what it is to be frail and strong at the same time. She shares the loneliness of missing someone and what it's like to fully love. Mostly, Annie shares with honesty and authenticity what it means to be human, painfully and beautifully human."

—**Christine Ristiano**, author of *"All the Silent Spaces"*

Annie's Song

Dandelions, Dreams and Dogs

Annie McDonnell

LU(ID
HOUSE
PUBLISHING

LU(CID
HOUSE
PUBLISHING

Published in Marietta, Georgia, United States of America by Lucid House Publishing, LLC
www.LucidHousePublishing.com
© 2023 by Annie McDonnell
All rights reserved. First Edition.
This title is also available as an e-book via Lucid House Publishing, LLC
Cover and interior design: Jan Sharrow
Author photo courtesy of Annie McDonnell

This book is a cross-genre blend of memoir, auto-fiction, and poetry. Some names and identifying details of certain individuals have been changed to protect their privacy.

Library of Congress Cataloging-in-Publication Data:

McDonnell, Annie, 1969-
Annie's Song: dandelions, dreams and dogs/ by Annie McDonnell—1st ed.
ISBN: 978-1950495351
e-book ISBN: 978-1950495368
1.Memoir 2. Grief and loss 3. Kidnapping 4. Best friend's murder
5. Long Island, New York 6. Ireland 7. Miscarriages 8. Medical mysteries
9. Misdiagnoses 10. Rape/Sexual Assault 11. Endometriosis 12. Hysterectomy
13. Infertility 14. Disabled Writer 15. Rare Diseases 16. Stiff Person Syndrome
BIO033000
FIC061000
POE023010

Pay It Forward

Proceeds from the purchase of Annie's Song will be donated to these charities.

I am a proud, longtime volunteer for **One Love Dog Rescue, Inc.** in memory of our boy, Simon, who was rescued from a kill shelter where he'd spent two years in a crate. I call the work I do #OperationSimon. My job within the group falls under fundraising and community outreach.

We are dedicated to rescuing dogs from all over the world and locally, even if they need healing from injuries, sickness, or abuse. We take dogs—not just the puppies—regardless of age, health, and the severity of the case. We rescue the entire family, which is why I chose to volunteer here. The founders, Cecilia McAloney, Nicole Oziel Slatky, and Lisa Christiansen and our team of volunteers do the complex work of coordinating dog rescues in disaster areas. The power of One Love Dog Rescue is found in the dedication and devotion of its volunteers to its mission: "One Love, One Heart, One Mission ♥ ♡ ♥" I am so proud to be part of this team. We all strive to ROCK the motto!

https://m.facebook.com/OneLoveDogRescue/

I am an online student at **The Muse Writers Center**, and I absolutely love it. This book would not exist without the center's classes. The fact that I could take entire classes online via Zoom made all the difference for me. The classes were hybrid with some students being in person and others like me online. I often got scholarships for classes or have been allowed to make monthly payments. One of the top 10 centers for writers in the nation, The Muse Writers Center stands alone in offering tuition assistance to anyone who wants to take a class but cannot afford it. Located in Norfolk, Virginia, near the Norfolk Naval Base, The Muse Writers Center offers creative writing classes and seminars to our US service members and veterans.

The Muse lives up to its motto: *The Literary Arts for Everyone*
About The Muse - https://the-muse.org

I've loved Pat Conroy's work ever since I discovered his books. As I learned more about him as an author and his dedication to mentoring students and authors just as he had been mentored, I loved him even more. I was shocked when Jonathan Haupt, executive director of the **Pat Conroy Literary Center**, asked me to hold an interview with him and tour of the literary center. I literally thought I was being punked because it seemed surreal. I asked him to let me teach some workshops on being a professional book reviewer and starting an online book club. He agreed and also agreed to have me interview him and his first intern Holland Perryman. The center holds many classes and produces online shows of interest to authors and writers of all skill levels. Most importantly, Jonathan and the center honor the late Pat Conroy's devotion to spreading his love of literature through teaching and mentoring emerging to advanced writers. It also offers scholarships and spaces for book clubs, writers' groups, and more.

"One can learn anything anything at all, I thought, if provided by a gifted and passionate teacher." —**Pat Conroy**

About The Pat Conroy Literary Center
https://patconroyliterarycenter.org/about/

Stiff Person Syndrome (SPS) is one of the many diseases I battle. Also called Tin Man's Disease, this rare disease has progressively taken away so many things from me, and it's woven into many of the essays and poems throughout this book. Some of my stories may be hard to read, because a lot of people are uncomfortable with the topics of serious diseases and death. I chose to share my journey because SPS needs more research to find ways to mitigate the symptoms and someday find a cure. **The Stiff Person Syndrome Research Foundation** was founded by Tara Zier, a young athletic mother and dentist whose symptoms appeared in the wake of her husband's tragic death. Like most of those of us with SPS, it took a while for Tara to get a diagnosis. The average diagnosis takes seven years.

I love the Foundation's mission: *Breaking through barriers to find a cure.*

About The Stiff Person Syndrome Research Foundation
https://stiffperson.org/

Thank you for purchasing this book and supporting causes that are all part of my heart and my story. Books saved me and gave me a family of readers, writers, and authors who have lifted me up in so many ways and encouraged me to fulfill my dream of writing the book that you are now reading. My rescue dogs and cats bring me so much joy and watch over me. We must advocate and be a voice for animals. They are counting on us. Finally, I ask you to help spread awareness of Stiff Person Syndrome, so that a cure can be found. Our voices and written words contain so much power.

Proceeds from this book in any format and resulting from any other medium in which these stories are shared will go to One Love Dog Rescue, New York; The Muse Writing Center, Norfolk, Virginia; The Pat Conroy Literary Center, Beaufort, South Carolina; The Stiff Person Syndrome Research Foundation, Bethesda, Maryland, as directed by Annie's wishes.

Dedication

With love to my supportive husband, Tom, and our dogs,
Daphne, Bonnie, and Sullivan,
and our cats, Bella, Mikah, Petra, Luna and Zero.
And in loving memory of my (step)Mom Carmela,
Best friend Jennifer, and beloved boy Simon.

People got sick of me being sick.
They simply stopped being in my life.
Just to be clear,
I am sick of being sick, too.
I just have no choice in the matter.

To the people who never left me,
To the people who always
included me in their life,
Even with my issues that seemed
to drive others away.

To the people who
always supported me,
I will always love you
just as unconditionally,
Thank you is not enough.
My gratitude is endless.
You are all part of my story,
as much as Tom and my pets are.

Like family,
You all offer me great love and hope.

I dedicate this book to all my loved ones,

Just turn the page,

and look for your name!

Table of Contents

Be a best friend.
Tell the truth.
Devour books.
Overuse "I love you!"
Do what brings you joy.
Do your best.
Be kind.
Smile.
Dance.
Never let your praying hearts get lazy.
and always love like crazy!

Love.
Annie

I Invite You to Experience "Annie's Song"

*M*y hope is that you don't just read this book. You experience it through the five senses.

Hear the songs that are attached to the QR codes at the end of every essay or poem. Each QR code takes you to a YouTube video with music that reminds me of what I wrote about or songs from that time in my life. You won't know the name of the song or band/singer until you view the QR Code. Once you click on it you will be directed to the YouTube video. At the end of "Annie's Song," you will find a Spotify QR code for my entire playlist.

Touch will be discovered when you are holding the book or your eBook tablet in your hands.

Sight will bloom in your mind as you read each piece. I hope that what I wrote gives you visions of dandelions and their seeds, crowns, dogs, love and hugs and kisses.

Smell comprises a key component of the five senses. Memories are often triggered by what we smell. I would love this book to come more alive for you through scent. Light a candle or incense with your favorite scent as you read these pages. If you read a tough part of the book, wash your hands and face with a beautifully scented soap to cleanse anything sad away.

Taste can be achieved with your favorite beverage as you read. Pour yourself a cup of tea or coffee or a glass of whatever you enjoy. Whenever I'm reading a good book, I like to give my dogs a treat.

"Annie's Song" is designed to be more than the words on the page, and by approaching it this way you'll discover the messages between the lines. I always envisioned this book expanding your idea of heaven and earth, and all the things in between, and helping you imagine what it is like to live in both places happily. That is my hope for you.

2

Her Name is Echo

Her name is Echo.
I wonder if her parents knew that her name would decide her destiny?
For she takes words and whispers them
to dance on the wind
and shouts accolades for others
from the rooftops,
Humble when it comes to hers.
All of the echoes ring in our ears to never be forgotten.
Echo always believes in her words
As strongly as an evening camper needs a fire.
Echo whispers encouragement to her writers.
When she cheerleads for you, you feel 100% wrapped in love
like a huge, warm sweater on a cold day.
Echo is innovative and loving and kind,
Her words will echo for many lifetimes to come.
Everything from Echo's mouth has meaning.
So, listen closely and intently, then repeat them.
To be Echo's friend is to know true friendship,
honest, forgiving, always trying to make each other better.
It is offering each other grace when we need it.
It is listening to your friend read their stories to you 500 times
and not complaining.

I'm grateful to Echo for a universe of reasons.
Whatever began our friendship, I cannot remember.
It was more magical, we just slipped into each others lives,
because it feels like she has always been with me.
Echo treats me like family, like part of her clan.
Echo has done so much for me,
the biggest has been believing in "Annie's Song."
Echo inspires me,
She moves me,
Echo is a champion to so many.
When your words evoke genuine emotion in Echo,
she will echo words so highly of you to everyone.
Echo has so much heart and respect for people
she loves and works with.
I am so blessed to be someone
Echo calls a friend.
My gratitude to her is immense.
My love for her is earnest.
Her name deserves to be honored.
For she is not just a whisper or a shout,
She is an echo dancing through so many lives.
Not only caring about her
Orange Duffle Bag Initiative,
But you and me and us!
For decades she has worked wholeheartedly to support
older children in the foster care system,
To inspire and give them hope for a better day and faith that they
can succeed.
Echo's words, work, and devotion to foster teens and young adults
changes lives.
I trust her heart and soul is proud like any mother would be.
Let's all speak of Echo,
The way she speaks of us.
Echoing words of Echo
Will open doors!
We could all use
An Echo in our lives!

Love note: The Orange Duffel Bag Initiative (ODBI), co-founded by my publisher Echo Montgomery Garrett, provides certified life-plan coaching and ongoing advocacy for students 14-24, who are experiencing homelessness, high poverty, and/or aging out of foster care. The 12-week program is based on a transformational change process: Sam Bracken's *7 Rules for the Road* found in "My Orange Duffel Bag: A Journey to Radical Change," Sam's graphic mini-memoir that Echo co-wrote. ODBI's award-winning, evidenced based program is built around sharing your story to create empathy and connection and then being coached to create a new story with caring, loving advocates by your side the entire way. Storytelling is at the heart of this Atlanta, Georgia-based nonprofit that has helped more than 2,000 high school and college students stay on track for educational success and achieve their goals.
About Orange Duffel Bag Initiative: https://theodbi.org/

♥ ♥ ♥

"You will know them by their love."
John 13:35

"Born to shimmer, born to shine."
—lyric from Shawn Mullins' Shimmer

"Books and ideas are like blood.
They need to circulate, and they keep us alive."
—Janet Skeslien Charles, "The Paris Library"

With Gratitude to My Teacher Diane Zinna

*D*iane Zinna is a talented author who shares her expertise with so many others. Her novel, *The All-Night Sun,* was my favorite novel of 2020.

Diane opens up our hearts and souls and helps us get what we need to onto the paper. Diane creates such a safe space for us that we are able to be completely vulnerable. This vulnerability leads to words and works that we never imagined we could create. Often, I have found myself dealing with an issue I had never been able to face before. It is so rewarding.

We all walk away from her classes knowing we have elevated our skill level. It's amazing what she does. Each of her students feels they are so important to her.

Diane helps create authors, whether it is the next generation of published authors or writers who want to write for themselves. Between her writing classes, literary support and grief writing Sundays, Diane has created a huge community.

Each student is always talking about how grateful they are to her. I am proud to be one of her students.

Diane Zinna was chosen as *The Write Review*'s Author Educator of the Year 2021.

This book exists because the majority of these essays and poems were written during her classes in response to prompts in about 15 minutes. Prompts help ignite your imagination to write about something. Diane's prompts always get my words flowing.

My gratitude to Diane is endless. She helped me deal with traumas that years of counseling still hadn't unraveled.

My Ars Poetica

Because I was born as an accident and feel like I ruined two lives and maybe more. Because I live in the sadness and grief being born of that accident. Because I'm still unloved. Because I was too young to witness my own family break up.

Because I went for the cookie jar at five years old and fell off the stove. It was decided we would never see my grandparents and uncle, who is my godfather, anymore. Because I was so lonely without them. Because I felt guilty for falling while they were babysitting. Because I let my siblings down. Because it is too much guilt for a five-year-old to bear. Because I always lived in guilt. Because the guilt hurt way too much.

Because my only getaway was going to Ireland over the summer if I got an A in every subject. Because those were weeks of respite for me. Imagine a child my age needing respite? Because I cried leaving Ireland. Because I loved it there. Because it felt like home.

Because I left Manorhaven, NY, in second grade, leaving behind one of my first very best friends, Stephanie. Because we never said goodbye.

Because we moved what felt like every year. Because it was usually during the middle of the night. Because I never knew when the next move was coming. Because I never had time for proper goodbyes with anyone. Because I never learned how to be in lasting relationships.

Because I told plenty of adults all around me that I was being stalked by a man whom I believed wanted to kill me and my best friend. Because no one believed us. Because they didn't believe me when I told them he tried to kill me on December 5, 1984, my fifteenth birthday, by luring me into the woods. Because he sexually assaulted and murdered my best friend on December 9th.

Because four decades later I still must write to the parole board, prison guidance counselor, my senator, district attorney, and Suffolk County homicide every two years when he is up for parole to keep him in prison. Because I write and call the newspapers, radio stations and news channels to get articles written about the parole hearing. Because I write a lot of press releases for social media. Because I must write to the Parents of Murdered Children to start their petition. Because I have to start a petition of my own.

Because Jennifer was only twelve years old, about to turn thirteen. Because she and I were Irish dancing partners and best friends. Because I stopped dancing when Jennifer was murdered. Because we were in a bad place when she died. Because I never said, "I love you." Because I was never the same. Because it felt like love always left me.

Because I learned I was a good writer at an early age. Because my first poem published was about a peach in first grade. Because I started reviewing books for the school newspaper in third grade. Because in sixth grade I won a March of Dimes writing contest and won money for college and a six-foot stuffed harp seal. Because children threw mud at me as I walked home from school with my brother. Because of jealousy. Because of anger. Because of heartbreak.

Because I was date raped in college and almost forced to have an abortion. Because I wasn't pregnant after all. Because I broke my neck in a car accident at age eighteen, and I had to leave college early. Because the driver, Tim and I had to break up. Because my heart broke from loving him so deeply. Because the better part of this story is that I received an honorary degree from college.

Because I was in an abusive relationship and got away thanks to Susan.

Because when I was twenty, I got custody of my sister. She was thirteen, and she's always hated me for it. Because I was never good enough for her, but I know I tried. Because I was a child myself. Because she compared me to grown adults, who already had their own children. Because all I did never mattered. Because she broke my heart. Because I saw us as being best friends, and she didn't.

Because my Navy boyfriend got injured during Desert Storm and almost died. Because I felt my guardian angel leave my body to go save him.

Because I was raped again in Richmond, Virginia, by a stranger. Because my new boyfriend questioned me about what I had done to provoke the attack, and I threw him out. Because I tried to commit suicide after that rape and breakup.

Because at age twenty-three I needed a total hysterectomy, which came about after years of nobody believing I was genuinely sick with endometriosis. Because I have fought this stigma ever since.

Because I had three miscarriages trying to get pregnant before my female parts were removed. Because there were no eggs to retrieve. Because I would never have my own child. Because God won't tell me what I did wrong.

Because I thank God my mom and dad found wonderful new spouses whom I could depend on and fall in love with properly.

Because I felt compelled to volunteer for Parents of the Murdered Children, at hospice and with the ambulance. Apparently, I suffered some form of hypervigilance, running towards the screams instead of away. Because this led to trust issues.

Because I was diagnosed with complex-post traumatic stress disorder (C-PTSD) with anxiety and depression and maybe a little rub of bipolar was stuck to my psyche. Because I tried every form of counseling you can imagine, with EMDR psychotherapy sending me to suicidal thoughts again.

Because my nephew was born with a heart defect that was fixed through surgeries, thanking God I was able to be there. Because that is what family does. Because I don't take my family for granted. Because I hate anyone who dares to make such an accusation. Because I wish I could write her name in charcoal just to watch it burn.

Because when I was thirty-one, I finally laid my eyes on the man I wanted to marry, and I manifested that because we are married now. Because we bought our own home when I was forty.

Because I entered a book review writing contest with *Elle* magazine and I was accepted as one of fifteen book reviewers. Because that was the best job I ever had.

Because that psychiatrist stuck his tongue in my mouth. Because he made nowhere feel safe.

Because I was my (step)Mom's caregiver the last nine months of her life. Because she was my dream of a mother with her sincere mushiness. Because she loved me as her own. Because my sorority sister Erica pushed me in a wheelchair for a marathon and a half by request of my (step)Mom's last wishes. Because I went to visit Mayo Clinic, Rochester, Minnesota, to try to discover what's wrong my health. Because my friends helped get me there. Because at age fifty I was told I should go into hospice, and Tom and I said "No."

Because I won a Lifetime Achievement Award. Because there was a book awarded in my name the same year. Because I was bullied online by a woman who I thought was my friend. Because some friends threw me to the wolves. Because I have the best of friends that make up for most of my family disliking me. Because my family always found fault in everything I did. Because God always gave me everything I needed.

Because I was loved.

Because I wasn't loved.

Because I am loved.

Because I loved.

Because I love dog rescue and the whole One Dog One Love Rescue family. Because being a Freedom Rider meant everything to me. Because I love promoting authors, and now it's time for me to promote myself. Because I love writing and hopefully at least a few people will love reading what I write. Because I finally stopped trying to prove myself to people. Because I learned the value of my love and if somebody didn't value it then they didn't deserve it. Because it took me many decades to learn that.

Because I know I'll meet my children in heaven. Because my husband Tom always takes care of me. Because I have the best dogs and cats, so I am indeed a mama. Because I got sick and became disabled too soon. Because I make the most of what I have to offer the world. Because of the way I walked a long and scary road at times. Because it was all well worth it. Because I think I'm kind of cool. Because I am not only a survivor, I am a warrior. Because I am the storm.

Because I'm so proud of being Irish and researching my ancestry. Because I love doing the same for my stepfather, who was adopted. Because I'm proud to be a Zeta Tau Alpha (ZTA) sorority sister. Because people believe in me. Because the ones who don't will be proven wrong. Because I love shamanism, God, and angels. Because I've been sick most of my life with some crazy rare diseases and I never give up. Because I'm still here.

Because even in death I hope to be remembered.

Because I hope to teach people to love and allow themselves to be loved, to be kind to one another and to have faith…because above all things, these are the most important.

Because I love the words extravaganza, extraordinary, mahalo, and Guadalajara, and I want to write these words as often as I can. Because I love dandelions and other weeds. Because I see so much in them. Because I make wishes on them. Because I root for the underdog. Because I see beauty where most people don't.

Because I want my books on the library shelves and in people's hands.

Because I have dreams to share.

Because I have a story to tell.

If "Annie's Song" Were Not a Book

*I*f "Annie's Song" were a celebration, it would be a retirement party because Annie is trying to say goodbye to everyone appropriately with love. There would be a guest book on the table. It would not be for guests to sign, but where each guest gets a private note from Annie who is surprising the guests with the fact that this party is for them, not her, to show her gratitude and how much she loved them for making her life so complete. She has nothing else to ask for. Having them in her life was like winning the lottery, only better. She was made rich by their love.

Like Annie's goodbyes at the celebration, you feel the love and sorrow collide. It's a new emotion to navigate around, but you notice Annie is not sad. She wishes you would not be either.

If "Annie's Song" were a tear, it would be wiped away by Annie's friends. Annie would look over and see a never-ending line of friends ready to wipe that tear, and all that may follow. These friends know she would walk the line to wipe their tears away, too.

If "Annie's Song" were a heart, it would be the sound of a soothing melodic lullaby instead of the tachycardic rhythm that can drive Annie's C-PTSD out of control. When Annie's heart beats like this she is scared to fall asleep. She has been told many times that she will most likely die in her sleep. Therefore, the lullaby is perfect. She just wants to be soothed. She knows she has lived a sanguine life.

If "Annie's Song" were an intravenous drug, it would be sure to heal many instead of not working at all. They keep increasing Annie's infusion dosage and it's not helping. The doctors refuse to administer the two alternative drug options, afraid the risks to Annie outweigh the benefits.

If "Annie's Song" were a quilt, it would be king size with each square made with love and care by her ZTA sorority sisters. They made it to wrap her in their constant and undeniable love since they can't always be with her. She feels their love tremendously.

If "Annie's Song" were a MOLST, we would tell the cardiologist he was wrong. Annie is not planning on dying within the thirty-day prognosis he gave her, and she is not going into hospice because she wants to fight even though the tests say her body is exhausted.

That was over two years ago. Annie and Tom were right about her strong will and iron constitution. Tom said she was too alive to be dying anytime soon.

If "Annie's Song" were a candle, it would light someone's path, pleasantly smelling of lavender, gardenias, and sandalwood—Annie's favorite scents. This special soul would find peace breathing in the candle lighting their path. This made it clear enough for them to be willing to face another day. There were times in Annie's life where she had a similar candle when she was lost.

If "Annie's Song" were a purse, it would have Annie's best friend's phone number on a card and some quarters in an envelope so she could call them. Her favorite color lipstick would be inside, too. There has always been something magical about lipstick to Annie, so feminine. No matter how unwell she is, lipstick has always made her look and feel beautiful.

If "Annie's Song" were a song, it would be about love and loyalty, for Annie wants to be remembered for her love and dedication to her friends and family. All she can leave behind is this. Love and loyalty are her legacy.

If "Annie's Song" were a dandelion, you could make one thousand wishes. You could offer the wishes to someone else because Annie learned that passing things forward is the best way to be. Paying any goodness forward, this is what makes the world go around in a delightful way. Annie may be in agony, but her soul is happy and joyful.

If "Annie's Song" were a dream, you'd be sound asleep on the most comfortable pillow, dreaming your life's most important dreams into reality. You'd know that manifesting is a thing! This is how she is married to Tom. She manifested their love.

If "Annie's Song" were a dog, you would be guaranteed unconditional love and support every moment it was by your side. You would never know what being alone feels like. You would always know what it was like to walk through the front door and find happiness and joy jumping all over you. There's nothing better. Don't ever take your dog for granted.

If "Annie's Song" were grief, the book would be soaked with tears for these words were written with sorrow, true love, and dignity.

Annie isn't one to let things hold her down. She has been through so much and has still lost even more, but she's determined to remember everyone for their love.

What you think about when you are forced to face death is ironic. You don't think about the death as much as you think about your life. Any song about her will be about her life. A place where she could put her pen to paper, and soak the pages with tears, if necessary. Sometimes a good healthy cry is needed.

Then put the book in places where people would pick up the book to read it, like a library, so they can learn how to survive various traumas with grace and dignity.

Annie's hope is for people to love themselves enough to celebrate their lives with people they love.

"Annie's Song" is hope, faith and love wrapped together. This is how Annie lived her life. Through tough times she would be smiling and laughing, or at least trying.

6

The Cairn Statue Is My Döppelganger

I feel caged. I'm feel caged like an animal, with open metal squares where doctors can poke and prod me. Feels like I'm only stones, heavy and hard to move. Cement.

The pain, the suffering. The anguish, the hardship. The trying to remember to be joyful. I'm still here. I often hear it's about attitude. If you are telling me that, I know you don't know me at all.

Trying to bend over in prayer, but then I get stuck, and I wonder if God is even listening. I'm crying and begging to be able to move, like a feather or leaf in the breeze. I can't take a step without a scream from my soul to the heavens because my body is full of slowly flowing veins and organs that don't speak to one another anymore. Not even to my brain. Not even to my throat anymore.

These stones no longer sit at the edge of the river feeling the comfort of the flow of fluid. Nothing is luxurious anymore. There is no longer the soothing feeling of a touch or even a surrender to a hug. Only doctors and nurses touch me now. A lot of friends don't even want to visit.

Family never came. It's been more than 2 ½ years since I was told the seriousness of my illnesses. They are killing me. Only my nephew Adam is coming. He loves me, no matter how I am. I cried as we made plans. Tears of happiness. I hold on to these people. Adam and Xander were to come this week, but I was too sick. My spasms looked like seizures and eating was too difficult. I don't want them to see me this way. They truly love me.

My diseases are closing my organs with veins running with thick blood not able to make it to where it needs to go quick enough. My veins are getting stiff with stenosis from mere thirst.

My loving heart is becoming a rock, but this is my biggest weapon against this hopelessness, so I am trying to keep it from getting worse. It helps my body fill with all that is necessary to keep my skin supple in this cage, so I don't feel like cement. With the aid it is giving, I do feel there is a slowing down of everything.

I feel like I am full of stones that are black and blue and gray. There are still some prettier stones that will turn the color of this angry sky, but I can no longer look up at it. It hurts too much to see the beauty in all this pain. Cover all the mirrors please.

I must bow down and give into this, that is the worst of all. I'm turning into a statue. One that is no longer lovely to look at. People just walk past me without a second thought. I feel like I'm on a shelf collecting dust, or on the street with pigeons sitting on me.

There will have to be a surrendering. There will also have to be gratitude for the wonderful life I have led. The truth is I have no complaints, but I'd like more time. Time where I can at least move.

Surrendering is not a giving in or a giving up. It is an acceptance. An acceptance no one is helping me with. I feel so alone with just a few accepting me as I am in the truth. Almost everyone says, "Oh, you'll be fine."

So even if my heart turns to stone and stops, my soul will not. Thank God I believe in heaven. It is the only solace I have each night as I close my eyes, snuggling my dog Sullivan.

I pray to never leave but have acceptance if I do. Knowing that I am free and no longer in this cage sounds so beautiful. I will fly away like a bird soaring toward the heavens.

I Could Have Saved Us

*A*s we sat on the plush carpet in front of Jennifer's closet that had full length mirrors, we were talking about what we imagined our first kiss would feel like. When you're looking in a mirror at someone and talking it felt more important for some reason. It felt like an official conversation. We talked like this often. These were the mirrors that we tried on dresses or veils and danced and sang in front of. These mirrors witnessed our lives. They saw Jennifer last in the house on December 9, 1984.

I wish I had them. They heard everything. I think of them often. I bet they'd whisper memories to me. Maybe I'd even hear Jennifer's voice. I believe important belongings in our lives carry a bit of us with them always. Touch an antique and tell me you don't understand what I'm talking about

I always imagined my first kiss would be with Ralph Macchio or C. Thomas Howell kissing me at a dance after they arrived late. I told Jennifer it would be at the top of the stairs while the Prince song "When Doves Cry" was playing. I found that song to be so romantic. I thought of kisses every time I heard this song.

It was everything, imagining love and kissing a boy. It would be like the whole world stopped. I'd dream of my new boyfriend holding a Boombox over their his head outside of one of my classroom windows with the song *In Your Eyes* by Peter Gabriel playing. We would kiss after I ran out of class.

My life was going to be an epic love story. Jennifer's would be, too. We were sure of it.

Jennifer asked me who I wanted my first kiss to be with, and I told her it was Michael who lived across the street from her. She told me she didn't believe me, because she thought I was in love with his younger brother Gregory. I was not.

She thought I had kissed Gregory already. She stared at me with her deep brown, piercing eyes in the mirror, her disbelief obvious.

I tried to look back at her just as assuredly as my words, but for some reason I couldn't stop giggling, I thought it was funny that she thought I had a crush on Gregory. So, we ended up having a big fight. As she asked me to leave her house. I was trying to explain about the night before we watched the movie when we played Spin-the-Bottle, neither Michael nor Gregory landed on me, so I didn't kiss anybody. I didn't understand why she was so angry.

She liked Michael, so she wanted me to like Gregory. This is what teen-age girls argue over. I was in shock because I was telling the truth. I was also in shock because I thought she liked Gregory. I was so upset that we argued.

This was when I learned girls can get angry at other girls very easily. It was my first real argument with a friend. I never wanted to have an argument again. I felt awful. I couldn't enjoy anything. I also learned that when I make someone a friend of mine, I really commit to them.

The ages we were, you still believe your life is going to turn out like a movie. She was expecting something like *16 Candles*, with Michael on top of a table with a birthday cake and a candle, and a kiss. We were living in the movies and books and our Irish dancing, not noticing as much as we should have what was going on around us. Except for our stalker. We noticed him. Too well.

We knew were being stalked, but nobody was listening to us. So, we tried to ignore it as best as we could. Everyone else was, so why shouldn't we?? Maybe we are imagining it, we'd try to reassure each other.

But he gave us the creeps. We believed he wanted to kill us.

I did call her on my birthday. I couldn't take it anymore. But my begging didn't matter. We didn't make up. I left her house walking home alone, and I saw Bobby. I thought, *"This is it. I'm going to die while Jennifer is mad at me."* On

December 5, 1984, the day I turned fifteen years old, Bobby offered me a bag of M&Ms. He knew M&Ms were my favorite chocolate and that it was my birthday. He tried to get me to go into the woods with him to have a conversation. I told him we were on a busy highway and nobody cares anyway so there was no need to go into the woods. I also told him that my mother was heading towards me to meet me so we could go Christmas shopping.

His mood changed, and I could tell he was going to let me walk away. But then he grabbed the pocket of my Jordache jeans. I thought he was about to pull me into the woods. I didn't know what he was doing exactly. My pocket snapped, and I ran like hell all the way home. I lost my breath. I called Jennifer and begged her to run if she saw him again. She said, "Okay." We hung up.

I never imagined that four days later Jennifer would go missing and eventually be found raped and murdered. Our twenty-six-year-old neighbor Robert Turley was found guilty of 2nd degree murder, 1st degree attempted rape and 1st degree sexual assault.

When I heard that our stalker, Robert, killed her it felt like my heart exploded into thousands of shards of colorful glass. For years I was told that this explosion was going to come together like a beautiful stained-glass window. Don't they know how expensive they are? The price has no ceiling. I still have not healed like a beautiful stained-glass window. The cost is too high. This is going to cost me the rest of my life. My heart often shatters like this, because of Jennifer's murder. I will never get over losing her. I scoff when I am told I should be over it by now. It is the love for Jennifer I can't get over. I feel bad for anyone who doesn't understand this.

When I lost her, I understood that loving each other is what we should have been doing. This argument was a huge waste of time. I lost those few precious days with Jennifer, never dreaming the loss would be permanent.

I should have told her, "I love you. I love you more than both Michael or Gregory or those movie stars all put together. I love you more than chocolate. Like the sticker you gave me."

What I learned through all of this was that Jennifer was my true first love. Our first love doesn't have to be a romantic one. It could be your very best friend, your person. The person you feel walking beside you even when they are not alive. My person was and is Jennifer. She is beside me. She protects me.

Jennifer never heard me say "I love you" the day she died. There is a lot of guilt in that.

The moment I feel anyone pull at my heartstrings now, I don't wait a minute to tell them I love them. Love is an essential bond between human beings. It is supposed to last a lifetime, just as it did with Jennifer. Love doesn't need to have such a huge price. It is the unloving that has the price.

Losing Jennifer taught me that you can always fight with your friends, but you certainly don't let arguments last. Any true friend will forgive your trespasses, and you, theirs. We should never expect perfection. To me, the loss is too great.

I get upset when I lose a friend, and some people think I'm crazy for that. But I know the price I paid for that one argument: never speaking to Jennifer again or hearing her laugh. I hate knowing that's bound to happen with more people in my life. People don't have to be dead for you to hurt terribly when you stop speaking.

I wish I crossed the street to the shopping center on December 9, 1984, between 2:30 and 3pm, instead of sitting in my home bitter and cold hearted, still stewing about being upset with you, Jennifer.

I'd always meet her, so she never walked alone because of Bobby—except for that one day.

I could have saved you.

I could have saved us.

What was I thinking?

8

Jennifer's Heartbeat

(To be read with Tchaikovsky, Symphony 6,

Movement 4, "Karajan")

My name is Jennifer, and this is the song of my heartbeat during my last hour here on earth.

I am an Irish dancer, so everything I do is in steps of eight, just like the music I play on my violin. I am also a cross country runner. I do the same thing when I run, constant counts of eight in my head. But there is no torture ever in it. This is all about love. It's the beat of my heart.

There is plenty of torture and screaming and yelling and pain and blood and scratches in my last hour. All fast, loud. powerful beats of eight. All of them hurt. All make me cry. All of them want to be heard. But no one is listening. No one ever did.

I can't slow him down!!

Bobby is the loudest, most painful music I've ever heard. I have always tried to be soft, lovable music everyone loved to hear.

What is this? I don't like it. This is too painful. This is not fair.

His sound is going to kill me, isn't it? This is not music.

He's making me become that same loud painful growl begging to be heard! Is anyone listening? We are both becoming very loud.

Let me back up, so you know how I got here:

I had just gone Christmas shopping, and it was so much fun. I was walking home from the mall. I was so happy. I just passed Annie's house. We are best friends. I love her. Have I told her this?

Then, I felt him behind me. Me and my best friend could always feel him. We didn't have to see him to know he was there. We would turn around, and his eyes were like that of a wolf, staring at us, like we were his prey. We were in big trouble. We knew it. No one was listening.

I started to run, counts of eight! Only think positive. I will get home. 1,2,3,4,5,6,7,8….I repeated this three times until he caught up with me and he pounded my head with a rock.

Then. Nothing.

There was just darkness, and I don't know for how long. Black. I was passed out. Dreaming. My mind tried to be my safety net.

My wedding day. I was so glorious. I had on a lacy white dress at the church, and my dad was walking me down the aisle. I could see my best friend at the end of the aisle, but I couldn't see who I was marrying.

I could see all the people who loved me. I counted my steps. 1,2,3…1,2,3. The music was like a lullaby. Was I awake? Was I asleep? Was I dead?

I can't see who I am marrying. I am walking closer and closer with loving heartfelt steps. I am happy here. I don't want to leave.

Oh no! I was dreaming. I am waking up!

I feel like I woke up so quickly! Sudden inhale of a deep breath. Bobby is on top of me. I am naked. What is Bobby doing? I don't understand! I'm so scared! This really hurts.

I am naked!!! This hurts!

That screaming! That scratching! The music is getting louder! Elevating! I'm scratching Bobby's face. The beats of eight for the music are all colliding; they're banging into one another!

Nothing is making sense.

I'm begging Bobby to stop!! It's because it hurts! It's because I'm scared! It's because I was only supposed to do this with my husband!! I hate him! It's because I'm so confused!!

Why is Bobby doing this to me!!! Why is Bobby still on top of me!!

Why can't anyone hear me screaming for help!!

Bobby is not looking at me anymore.

I think it's over, but it's not.

My last crescendo! I scream as loud as I can.

Bobby wraps my belt around my neck.

I must now give in. I try to just think of my family and friends, the music beats are getting softer…or are they going backwards? I don't know?

The music is so soft.

I don't think I'm thinking straight! Where is my best friend? Why isn't she helping? Where is my family??

I can't scream anymore.

The music stops.

I can't tell what's happening. Can you tell me? Can anyone tell me what's happening?

It is over.

I'm only 12.

Cloak and Dagger

Grief wraps my heart like a cloak and dagger, often the perpetrator of my pain. But more often the savior of mine.

Last night it helped my heart keep beating when Jennifer was missing after school. I could feel each beat, loud, sounding like a drum ready for battle. It was flowing through me. Hard, desperate, and powerful. My grief was preparing me for war.

Jennifer was my best friend and was shopping at a small shopping center along the highway across the street from my home, and just a few turns to her house.

I felt the cloak tighten. I know this war is going to be with Robert Turley, the 26-year-old who has been stalking us. I wanted to call anyone that afternoon and tell them that he had been stalking us, but I was terrified.

I heard Jennifer was dead. I heard he tried to rape her or maybe he did, I don't know. I need to start carrying a picket sign that says: *Listen to your children before it's too late. .*"

The cloak pulled so tightly it would never let me go for the rest of my life. My heart is pierced by a dagger, so I think I'm constantly bleeding this pain. Because I will write a lot about all the grief in my voice, words, and not being able to speak properly.

I am always ready to hurt anyone even looking like they might hurt me. I am always on alert. It feels like pounding rain pouring on me, and I can't get away.

I just want to leave. This is such a burden to bear. The moment I wake up in the morning I just burst into tears because I don't want to repeat the day. I know Jennifer will be part of it because she always is. No one wants to be around this cloak, no, no one wants to be around this dagger.

I didn't do it to myself. This was done to me. Yet, I am treated like a disappointment by some for having issues with trauma and grief. I am expected to be "over it." All I know is that I am not offered empathy or compassion. I am obviously deeply and profoundly wounded emotionally.

Where is the grace?

Robert's parole hearings are in August. They began after his first twenty-five years of incarceration. Every two years after that, I must recount how I was the lucky one who got away.

The scars of grief I carry have cut so deep. We never should've been stalked. We could've been protected. Jennifer certainly should not be dead. I should not spend any time wishing I was killed instead.

The dagger is my tool to feel protected.

The cloak is also my protection.

It is my hug from Jennifer.

Not everything has to hurt.

Tears for Jennifer

W hile speeding down the expressway, sitting in the backseat of my father's car, I was stunned by the beauty of what is called Queen Anne's lace lining the exits. I later found out that it was considered a weed. There must be something between me and weeds. I always fall in love with them. Maybe it is that they are considered "less than" flowers, but they are just as beautiful. Only certain people seem to notice their beauty and appreciate all they can offer. Kind of how I feel about myself, in a good way.

Each plant was so intricately beautiful and appeared soft and holy. For some reason, I felt they were to be revered. The sight of them made my heart skip a beat as we whizzed by.

In the wake of my twelve-year-old best friend Jennifer's murder, whenever my tears flowed, they gave me flashbacks to those fields of Queen Anne's lace. It made no sense. Thirty-six years of tears later since her death, I bet I could look under the microscope at my tears and still see that Queen Anne's lace.

I never knew that tears were original like snow and icicles, but of course they are! Each person is as original as the reason for their tears just as each Queen Anne's Lace is original.

My crying for Jennifer would feel like my body screaming out loud. Like a car rushing down an expressway, always getting off at that exit. Yet, looking around and seeing that elegant field of original flowers. I thought they would make the most beautiful bouquet to bring home, but I never stopped to pick any. I cannot bear to get too close. The thought made me too emotional.

Like touching grief, not only feeling it.

This weed belonged to no one. Grief was everyone's and no one's at the same time. Maybe when children died all the tears look like this delicate quilt of Queen Anne's lace. Fields and fields of them fill the otherwise barren spaces. They look so delicate, like snowflakes that melt when you touch them. I doubt hardly anyone tries to bring a bouquet home.

They are all white, reminding me of the color of Jennifer's casket and the color of the flowers surrounding the funeral home for her wake and the church during her funeral. I imagine her gravesite had white flowers surrounding her burial plot. I was not able to go there at the time. I couldn't bear to see her being put into the ground.

That was too much for me to handle. I was nowhere near ready for those tears at age fifteen. I was grieving Jennifer's death alone. I needed guidance, and I never got it. I was alone attending anything in honor of Jennifer. I went to her services with another family. I felt invisible—overlooked by virtually everyone just like Queen Ann's lace.

I think the adults around us bore so much shame from ignoring our warnings about Robert. We knew he was stalking us. Who wants to believe children saying a neighbor is stalking them? Especially, when we'd add, "He is going to kill us."

Four days before Jennifer was murdered, on my birthday, he tried to get me into the same wooded area where he killed Jennifer. We were repeatedly told we were making a big deal out of nothing. He couldn't harm us. Until he did, and it was too late.

I imagine my tears for Jennifer to be beautiful. A crying out for her could only be a letting go of all the exquisite years I imagine I am missing with her and the wondrous things we've missed doing together like the white wedding gowns and veils that we weren't able to shop for together or lace up on the day of our weddings.

My tears are full of love. My tears send messages to Jennifer.

You never realize how delicate life is until it's gone. When you look at the Queen Anne's lace you see it is just as delicate. Tears are delicate like this, too. They disappear just as easily, don't they? Everything beautiful and loved should be cared for properly.

Who knew that someone other than God would take Jennifer away from me and us? Is this why her field of tears looked holy to me? Is this where she has gone? I can see her running and dancing in a field of these glorious weeds. I see dandelion seeds flying as she dances, too.

I have yet to look closely at Queen Anne's lace, but my tears reveal their delicate beauty to me, Next time I see something that's taking my breath away, I'm going to stop and look at whatever it is. I believe I was getting a message the first time I saw the field of these, only I wasn't ready to receive it.

I am not ready to face the legitimacy of my tears or Jennifer being gone. Stalking, abduction, sexual assault, and murder are seared into my memory.

I'd rather think of this field of soft, tiny, glistening white petals and imagine Jennifer there, because remembering her life is what I should be thinking of. Her laughter, her smile, her love, our friendship, our holding hands when we danced.

Not her last hours. Not the pain, the suffering, the feeling alone, the reaching for me....and, I wasn't there.

When all her greatness floated into the air up to heaven on angel's wings.

And the Queen Anne's lace wept tears for Jennifer before I even knew she was gone.

My Roe v. Wade Experience

Choices. Life changing choices. *I choose you*, I say to my womb. I say this silently as my mother drives me to meet the man who date-raped me at college.

My rapist and his parents were waiting at the abortion clinic. It was sickening. We are all waiting for the outcome of my pregnancy test, and they are all ready to make sure I kill it.

I do not want to kill my baby.

He will not be a father. Ever. At least not in my lifetime. He had a choice, and he decided to rape me. I thought he loved me. My college girl naivety, thinking anyone would understand my choices when it came to sex or abortions. I'm too young, and I'm still in college but I do have a choice. My CHOICE was to wait until I was married. Our choices should never be taken away. Especially not in this vile, forcible, truly unkind, and humiliating way. Let alone all the pain and suffering. I will never forget that pain.

Or his name. Or his hand over my mouth.

I had dreams to be an entertainment lawyer and to study at in the University of California at Berkeley.

He stole those dreams. He stole so many dreams in one night.

As we drive to the clinic, I roll the window down for some air. As I breathe in, I feel heartache. As I breathe out, I try desperately to let go of the dark memories haunting every neuron in my brain.

The drive to the clinic is torture. My mom told John's family that they had to pay for the abortion if I was pregnant. You see, I hadn't had my period in months. *This is beyond crazy that I am being forced to see him again.*

I was terrified that I was pregnant and that they were just going to basically rape me again by making me do it. Make me have an abortion.

Choices. These life-changing choices should be mine and only mine. Not my mother's and, most certainly, not his or his family's. I'm imagining a new life choice. Keeping this baby. Reading and singing this tiny being to sleep. I have so much love to give. Knowing that I'm smart enough to still become a lawyer, no matter what people keep telling me. Everyone is demanding an abortion. I was raped and had no choice as I screamed NO.

I certainly am convicted in this choice. I choose you. I say YES to you.

I'm being treated like nothing monstrous happened to me. Like we are in some sort of Sunday drive. Shut that music off.

Choices. These life-changing choices. I tell my mom as we approach the clinic that I will not have an abortion. We fight. She is yelling.

Choices. Life-changing choices. I tell my mother the solid answer for me is NO. I keep telling my belly that I want her and not to be scared. I will protect her, always.

We arrive and I am literally being pulled out of the car because I don't want to leave it. I don't want to face him, and I certainly don't want to face aborting my baby. It feels like I'm being raped all over again.

I close my eyes, and I imagine the ocean. Just like when he forced himself.... the waves crashing loudly.

We are all in the office where these choices are made all the time. I'm grateful each woman has their own safe choice to make, and I do believe it is every woman's right. I also believe it was mine to make that morning. I don't know what I would've done if I hadn't been raped, and I did not have a choice for yes and a safe choice for me to say no I cannot have this child.

Only I wanted her.

Choices. Life-changing choices. I choose you, but you are NOT there. It was most likely endometriosis and stress holding my period back.

I was holding an empty womb, all this time. I find that hard to believe, but it's true. I thought you were there and if you were, I thank God I had a choice. I am missing you and you were never there.

I thank God my friends who had abortions had a safe choice.

Choices. Life-changing choices just because I would've chosen to keep my child doesn't mean every woman would or should.

Choices.

Life-changing choices. Don't all women deserve to make their own choice?

Sharp Edges Turn into Love

I walk through this world
Imagining my days just going in circles.
free and happy and loving.
Instead there are sharp edges.
that hurt and sting and make my heart bleed.

I walk through this world.
Believing my loved ones are holding me strongly.
loving and supporting and defending.
My true and chosen family.
Not blood. not sworn to me. not obligated.

I walk through this world.
Knowing those sharp edges might hurt.
But. I am never alone.
My chosen family is behind me.
giving me their shoulders to lean on.

Sharp edges turn into love.

Love on Route 58

My life's dreams were over before they even began—crushed by a thirty-second malfunctioning of an 18-wheeler driving on the opposite side of the highway. The driver lost control, and his trailer came sliding across the opposing lane of traffic like a hockey stick trying to make a goal. The truck pushed aside every car in its wake until our car was stuck right underneath. We thought it was death, and it proved to be the death of a life Tim and I had planned.

Our weekend getaway began on a beautiful sun-filled Friday in 1989. Most of my ZTA sorority sisters were heading off to Ocean City for spring break. I couldn't afford to go with them, let alone take the entire week off from work. My sneaky boyfriend Tim asked my boss if I could have the weekend off, so he could take me to Virginia Beach to visit my mom. I hadn't seen her since my parents divorced, and he seemed to think I needed to see her. Plus, we could visit a beach!

We left High Point College in Tim's big ole southern boy truck, but I asked if we could drive his Mazda RX7. I told Tim that I felt safer in it. Truth was that my intuition told me something bad was going to happen to us if we stayed in that country truck.

We were rolling down that four-lane divided highway blaring the songs we loved from Guns N' Roses and Debbie Gibson. We came upon beautiful grassy area of Route 58, and then we saw a huge morbid sign declaring this 22-mile strip from Courtland to Emporia, Virginia, as the dangerous "Suicide Strip." The strip averaged one accident every six days between 1970 and

1991, with 100 deaths and over 1,000 injuries. We were confused by this kind of welcome.

Our initial reaction was burst into nervous laughter. I think a bit out of fear but we could find the humor in almost anything. This was Tim's shortcut. I was ready to smack him between giggles for taking us through the Suicide Strip.

I was wearing my ZTA sorority tank top, and Tim kept looking at my ZTA letters. He was blasting the song "Eternal Flame." Tim was in his PKA fraternity shirt and khaki shorts. My High Point College sweatshirt was tossed the backseat with my scrunchies, headbands and Kaepa high top sneakers and thick white socks.

Tim had made a mix tape for the trip. He was watching me and the road while I was singing and seat dancing. We were like that romcom couple that finally gets together at the end of the movie. Then, all at once Tim yelled "ANNIE!" I looked up to see this huge tractor trailer coming our way from the other side of the highway. It was slamming into cars and throwing them into the ditch on the side of the road like they were bowling pins.

All in extra slow motion. "I–get–lost–in–your–eyes" …the music is slowing down, too. The music was all I heard. Tim put his right arm in front of me to help brace my body for impact. In that moment I truly knew how much he loved me. We had not said "I love you" to one another yet, but I learned why people always say "actions prove love more than words." Tim loved me as I loved him. That was the kind of protection a girl like me had always been looking for. Now, in the blink of an eye, I wished I never needed it.

We were alone in this strange world where people were running around helping everyone but us. "They have to be dead," we heard people say. "Go help the others. We will get to them last." Tim and I kept telling each other that we were indeed alive. His nose was hanging off his face to one side. The rear-view mirror was hanging by its wires, so I tore it down. I couldn't let Tim see his face; it was so scary.

I kept saying "Oh my God" over and over. Tim tried to calm me down. We were each other's saving grace inside that vehicle. I had to get him to hold his nose on his beautiful still handsome face. Tim had to stop me from hyperventilating. Through all of it, I still see his eyes watching me calmly. The eyes of love can rescue you from the deepest moments of despair, and Tim's eyes spoke to me. To be each other's rescuer became our job because no one believed that we could possibly still be alive.

But we were alive, right? We didn't have enough strength to scream so people would hear us. Our words were faint whispers. The accident happened at about 3pm, but we were not pulled out from under the trailer until at least 5pm. Everyone was in complete shock that we were alive. We were both covered in blood and in utter agony. I didn't know where all the blood on me was from, but my neck and back were killing me.

The jaws of life had to be used to get us out of the car. We held hands. I looked into Tim's eyes and for a moment in time they took me away to the ocean. Then the rescue workers got him out.

I was alone, and my knee was stuck in the glove compartment. Then I was screaming and crying and begging them to get me out. My security blanket had been ripped from me. *Where is Tim?* They had to take the hood off to get my knee out. Then a strange thing happened. A lady handed me his fraternity cap and said, "Tim wants you to have this until he is with you again." How well he knew me. He knew I needed a piece of him.

They pulled me out of the car and put me on this hard stretcher, but my legs were still in a seated position. My body was in such shock that they wouldn't move. The rescue workers tied sandbags to my legs. They were still up in the air, but I was assured they would slowly come down. They finally came down a few hours later, inch-by-torturous-inch. The pain was intense.

I often imagine my life without this pivot. What might have been if that truck never got in our way on Route 58. Tim was the best boyfriend I ever had. I truly thought he was my man at the end of the aisle. I'd named our children. I'd imagined our life together. I often think of Cher's song "If I Could Turn Back Time" when these memories flood my mind.

Today I can still see his eyes looking at me from the seat in the Mazda. The ache in his eyes wasn't so much physical as it was an emotional heartache. Our life was splintered in the moment. Severed. Sometimes I wonder if my life afterwards was some sort of punishment for having survived but losing the love of my life. It's weird how a "can't have him" at age nineteen turns into a lifelong obsession of searching for your happiness again.

I used to tell him I could get lost in those crystal blue ocean eyes of his, Then suddenly his eyes were bleeding and we were trying to not drown in a river of red. It was the sudden severity of the loss, the intensity of the pain, in the knowing this was our last day. The fun, the carefree spirit of it all, was over. Everything moving forward would hurt, cut, and strangle me.

I had met my soul mate, and a 3M 18-wheeler swallowed our relationship like a spaceship coming to take its species home. We disappeared so fast, it was like lightning. I could feel and yet felt numb at the same time. I felt as though I was trying to swim in waves crashing against the shore during a hurricane. Too fast to breath or think and begging for a lifeguard to rescue you. The impact of this crash hurt so badly that I cried for decades. Crying tears falling in search of Tim.

Only later did we learned that if we had been in his truck, we both would have died. My intuition was why he switched vehicles, and we ended up under the trailer instead of being decapitated.

There are other things that have followed both of us in life that feel like another sort of decapitation. My life with Tim came to an abrupt end. My good health was certainly over. The head I was left with had a mind of sadness and depression. I was such a jubilant person until that day in 1989.

I try to summon that joyful girl back, but she is long gone. The impact of the Mazda and the truck made that girl disappear. All that was left was a shell of me. She died, leaving tears on paper that created words so sad and depressed. After that fateful day, putting pen to paper always felt like writing an obituary. There was now a constant storm where there used to always be sunshine. I needed an umbrella to get through my life. I needed protection. I was no longer safe. I trusted nothing.

Now I have finally been diagnosed with a disease called Stiff Person Syndrome. That fright never left my body. It took over. I still feel the weight of those sandbags when I can't move. Three decades cannot erase the trauma inside your body. That fact amazes me.

Even more amazing is what I can endure. I survive this crash repeatedly in my mind. My life is a million of these crashes. A billion of these screams and tears. I didn't know it in that moment, but I was scarred for life. More than a wound, I'm still open and bleeding. Life was about to get worse.

We were separated, because he was flown by helicopter to the big hospital in Richmond, and I stayed at the small Emporia General. He needed immediate surgery. I'd see him soon. We were so young to experience this trauma together. It's like a marriage. You become bound for life. You make a silent contract to stay together always because of this shared experience.

There will always be this mapping in my life that revolves around Tim and this accident. My connection to him is so profound and beautiful. I trust Tim, and I will always be in love. When I was going into hospice this past year, he was the first person I called. That's how strong our bond remains. Is he my person?

I broke my neck during that accident. Only recently did the doctors discover that the spinal fluid from the break of my C-7 vertebrae leaked into my bloodstream and must have caused an infection. That leak was overlooked and never treated, so I now carry several illnesses and fight for my life daily.

My chronic pain and illnesses serve as a constant reminder that we were meant to die that day. God had plans for us, and I changed them by insisting we switch vehicles. Is God angry that I did that?

Our goodbye was never a wanting or a needing. It was a cut, a slice, a severing. A physical cutting apart of two people who still loved each other. A pivot. A death.

My dream of marrying Tim ended that day. My dream of becoming an entertainment lawyer ended that day. My dream of being a mom ended that day. My dream of walking and dancing through life ended that day.

I think Tim and I still live in the seats of his Mazda RX-7 under the 18-wheeler looking at each other, never wanting to look away. This is a hard way to live. One foot in the past and one foot in the here and now.

A part of me died that day. A part of my heart left my body, and I have not been the same since. If I catch an image of myself in any rearview mirror, I don't recognize the girl looking back at me.

Each time I get a flare, or I am diagnosed with anything new, I flash back to this moment. I hear the music and I see Tim in the car and on the stretcher. I am stuck in that memory, and it plays on repeat in my mind.

Imprint Me with Your Love

Nothing ever being good enough,
not being able to have children,
trying always to be perfect in other ways instead,
but it never quite worked out.

Always loved less than.

I was born into a thirst and cry for love,
and that feeling has still not left me.
Was I born with this need for love, or did I grow into it?

Feeling like I was always in a head-on collision with emotions,
that is about to hit full impact,
ashamed of wanting to be heard,
I am always tense, waiting for the big crash.

For the moment the unloving begins.

I don't think I ever felt grounded until I moved to High Point College.
To be able to be myself all the time was unbelievably satisfying.

There's a certain comfort level that comes with
being in full control of my own life.
and I savored it.

It is said that I am hyper-vigilant to help people,
even if it causes jeopardy to my own self-care.

While I searched for love,
I tried to plant it everywhere.
I have a strong sense of abandonment issues.

I have learned that not telling Jennifer
that I loved her before she died
created a hunger inside of me that I cannot satisfy.

My (step)Mom was aware of this insatiable need I had,
because she cared to know me without shame.
She made sure I never questioned her love for me.

She and I imprinted on one another,
she needed the love I was offering
as much as I needed hers.

I needed to talk,
and be open about my feelings,
without being shut up,
or called a Drama Queen.

We were a perfect match:
mother and daughter,
daughter and mother.
Always.

My drama was wanting to love,
and be loved.
She loved that about me.

I loved that about her.

Come imprint me with your love,

I promise I will answer.

Sending the Man I Loved Off to War

Written in response to Porter Robinson's "Sea of Voices"

*J*ay and I walk hand-in-hand on January 8, 1991. I'm crying, not wanting to let go and I'm so scared for what he's about to do. He is comforted by and proud of his choice to join the U.S. Navy and serve our country. He's also deeply in love with "his boys"— specially the service members who work on the deck of the *USS Roosevelt* with him. I don't remember ever feeling so proud to be an American.

My best friend and roommate, Susan, was with us. I was so grateful that she could hold me together once Jay was gone. We were going to follow this ship until we could not see it at all. I wanted to watch it become part of the horizon as the *USS Roosevelt* headed down the Chesapeake Bay from Ocean View in Norfolk, Virginia

I am trying to get Jay to walk slower to the gate entrance of the ship, because I'm not ready. The bells are welcoming them to the USS Roosevelt, as this huge city on the sea sways in bay. Five thousand members are loading up.

My life. My dream. My Naval man in the green shirt is about to go fight in the sandbox from the sea. He keeps assuring me this assignment keeps him safe and nothing can happen to him on the ship. He is not on land, so he's not fighting on the ground. "Annie, it's okay. I'm sending planes off the flight deck. I'm 100% safe!"

I have the strangest feeling and was so uncomfortable letting him go. *What is wrong with me?*

This is my first close experience with war, and I'm terrified. I know what is asked of our military, and I know what is asked of us back home who love these men and women. *Am I ready?* I didn't even consider this before I began dating him.

Susan said I must be prepared for my heartache until he's home again on American soil. He kisses me goodbye, we hug for a long time, then we hold hands until we are so far apart, they drop by our sides. I know this is it.

My heart breaks.

This is my last look in his gloriously beautiful eyes. This is the last time I will see that tilted grin he has that I fell in love with when we first met on the steps in front of my condo. I left my heart right there at the pier.

And I watch him walk like a force of nature through the gate, like he is walking on water. I see him saluting a lot of people. The seriousness of this morning is not forgotten by me.. I am terrified.

The all begin to crowd at the top of the flight deck where he told me to look for him. I scan for Jay. The men are all lined up and saluting. This hurts way too much. My heart is breaking. *Is that even possible?*

This is such a profound moment in my life. I'm only 22. We are so young. I want to marry him. *Does he know that?*

Please God, bring him home safely. I can't stop praying. I am hysterically crying. Susan is trying to console me.

I can't find Jay. *Please don't pull away until we see one another again.* My silent prayer for that last glimpse goes unanswered.

F-14 fighter jets do a fly by.

This is it. They're pulling away. "Can't Cry Hard Enough" drifts through my mind.

I'm sending the man I love off to war. *Does he know I love him?*

We run to the tunnel to watch the ship leave port until it disappears on the horizon. My heart shatters with my last view of the *USS Roosevelt*. It will not be whole until Jay is back home.

On February 20, I am awakened from my sleep with this big cry and feeling as though my guardian angel has left me. I know she is going to help Jay.

I had a dream he'd been seriously injured, and I run and wake up Susan to tell her what had just happened. Of course, she thinks I am crazy. Then Jay's mother calls and lets me know he has been injured and is being treated and will be home. But she's not sure when.

The most amazing thing about all of this is what his Captain tells me, Jay was sucked to the intake of the A-6E plane that he was helping to catapult off the *USS Roosevelt*'s flight deck. His commanding officer says, "Nobody has ever survived this, but he was pulled out by something, like an angel pulled him out,"

"I believe with all my heart it was my guardian angel," I say.

"I believe that," the Captain replies solemnly.

My love for him was so strong my guardian angel knew he had to survive. If not for me, then for himself and another love and to become a father and grandfather.

Jay and I didn't last as a couple, but we are still in touch. I adore his wife, Lorie. She loves him so wonderfully, and that makes me so happy. When you love someone, you can let them go and move on.

On February 20, 2022, we honored his thirtieth Alive Day with my interview with Jay, Lorie, and author Carol Van den Hende at *The Write Review* on Facebook. Carol's award-winning novel, *Goodbye, Orchid* reflects upon many injured U.S. veterans, their sacrifices, their families and caregivers and all the love shared. All the decisions we choose to make after an injury during combat change the circumference of our lives, just as the accident itself did. We are reminded that in all this there is love of self and one another that sees us through. Today we celebrate Jay for all he has endured and sacrificed and his wife for always being by his side. We celebrate his life. They are blessed to have one another!

I was blessed to love Jay when I did. He taught me a lot. He is a survivor and a hero, although like so many veterans his humility causes him to dispute being a hero.

Interview with Jay

Crossroads

Once you take the wrong curve in the road
You look back often.
Crossroads are everywhere.

If you look hard enough
You will see me,
Standing there still.

Waiting.

You pump through my veins
You have always been in my heart
Part of me…Part of you…
Always standing at the crossroads.

We were good at loving
We were good at playing

We were good at everything
This lives in my heart.

You will always be the man there.
Standing at the end of the path,
The path I loved
The memories I live with.

Feel me.
Breathe me.
Fill me.
Never forget me.

Don't ever leave me.
Never unravel the road I am on.

I still live in the crossroads
And it keeps me happy.

We don't end,
We are a never-ending road.

Love can change
But hearts don't.

You were my other road.

There Is No Heartbeat

One day Savannah became more restless, and then there was nothing. I ignored the nothing. I was not willing to accept this void.

I had always worked hard to keep her calm by reading books to her, listening to music, singing, always massaging my belly.

I was being a mother. I wanted my child to know peace. I know what stress can do to children.

Today, I was walking. I was making sure that she felt movement and entertainment, too. I wanted her to always be in a state of relaxation and had a disdain for anything toxic. I dealt with too many anxiety-ridden things, and I did not want this for my daughter. I was starting her introduction to a calm life early.

When the doctors told me she was gone. I heard songs to her in my head. There was no heartbeat. I heard the songs louder.

I told them the reason we were not feeling her was because she was relaxing. They had to be wrong. I did not lose Savannah Alexis. I still felt her inside me.

We went home, and I read her a story.

Apparently, I was having a false pregnancy, My daughter was gone yet I was still convinced I was pregnant.

What is wrong with these people? I'm her mother! I know she is with me!

Then, the huge effort to convince me that my daughter had died in my womb began.

I felt attacked. I did not want to hear anything they were saying. I was slapped across the face, and it was like an awakening to the truth.

What is this emptiness I am feeling way too young? It's my heart that is feeling it and breaking.

At this point I feel like I am losing my mind. I am so angry. I am seething. All I keep thinking is "Take this uterus out ASAP"! I hate it. It has killed three of my babies. But keep everything else so I can freeze eggs. My new plan is a surrogate. I can't believe I'm even thinking this. But I cannot imagine not having a plan.

My memories seem to get a little lost here. To the best of my recollection, I needed a DNC. She was dead. At five months gestation. DEAD inside me. This could not be happening.

You can't imagine the wailing that came out of me. I think I knew it was true the whole entire day but for some reason I still believed she was alive. So, I don't understand how I was actually feeling her, It was confusing.

I could not face the loss. I'd imagined our life together too much. I had plans for us.

There was no heartbeat!

Losing Savannah Alexis gave away part of my heart. We had a nursery set up with lots of books. I was going to be reading to her all the time. I had lots of interactive things for us to do together, because I had waited my whole life for her. I had a lot of pink clothing, most things were handmade and everything was beautiful. I was gonna have a pretty-in-pink little lady.

I had endometriosis, and it took me forever to get pregnant. She was my last chance before my total hysterectomy. My uterus had spots of endometriosis so as the babies grew inside of me, they eventually got to an area where there was no uterine wall for them to attach to and I would lose them.

I had already had one possible miscarriage and one early miscarriage. I believe the early miscarriage was a boy we named Canyon Joseph.

After losing her, I knew I would never be a mother. She was my last attempt at pregnancy. I was never going to carry a child to term and give birth. I couldn't wait to hear her cry the day she was born. So many dreams died this day. Did I forget to wish on the dandelion for her?

How will I live my whole life without her? I hope she walks beside me, because when you lose a child, each day feels like Unmother's Day.

No celebrations. No joy. A lot of crying.

I am not the same woman. I am broken. No one can fix this. No one can love me enough through this.

No one is trying to love me through any of this.

Whenever anything happens to me it is always just pushed under the rug, and we move on. I cannot even take a moment to feel sorrow. No time to grieve. So, I really don't know if love can help you through difficult times with a loss this big. I've never had anyone to love me through anything. I only know facing loss alone. I didn't know how to grieve properly.

I always feel alone and ashamed to have emotions.

I trust she is with her brother. I will be with them when I go to heaven. That is the only solace that exists.

18

Womanhood Erased

I wake up from what should have been the removal of my uterus and the retrieval of eggs to freeze.

I signed that "just in case" paper because I was told the chance of removing everything was so slim. The chance of zero eggs, even slimmer.

I am lying in a hospital bed in Richmond, Virginia. These sheets are uncomfortable.

No one stops by to see how I am, emotionally or physically.

I am only 23, feeling more like a child than an adult.
I need to be comforted.
Devastated and in pain, feeling empty.
Alone.

My eyes aren't even fully open yet.
And I'm told one of the most profound things in my life.

A doctor walks in to tell me all my female parts are gone.
From womb to ovaries to fallopian tubes and cervix,
Worse yet, I'm told there were zero eggs to freeze.

Broken dreams flash before my eyes
as tears roll down my face.
No one hands me a tissue.
I stare at the sterile wall as I'm told I am in medical menopause.
Feeling instantly old. What are they saying?
I stop listening.

Endometriosis killed my womanhood,
it was really caused by all the doctors denying my illness

They called me a hypochondriac.
They just may as well have removed my soul.

What will ever matter to me now.

My voice once again being silenced.
No one listening as I cry out to be heard.
This is a pattern.

Lithium, Prozac.
Drugs given to me because I was considered a hypochondriac for five solid years.

Now I sit here in this uncomfortable bed, grabbing the blanket so tight, willing time to rewind.
Praying and wishing someone had heard me sooner.
This is their fault. I could have been treated with the proper diagnosis.

But who listens to women?

Flowers arrive from my three surgeons and the anesthesiologist.
They must feel guilty.
I learn I woke up in the middle of the surgery and tried to get off the table.
I knew they were erasing my womanhood.
I knew I didn't want them to continue.
I remember screaming "NO," yet no one heard me.

Everything goes from red to black and white.
All the color in my life has been drained out of me.
Anger to numbness back to anger.
Even hate.

I may as well have died on that operating table.

I'm breathing fire like a dragon.

I'm already having my first hot flash.
My skin is sweating as profusely as the rain pouring down the large

hospital window.
I want to stand in the storm and disappear into the crowd below.

I'm furious and sad and lonely.
I want a hug or a hand to hold.
A simple loving touch.

Everything starts to smell like gunmetal.
The steel taste in my mouth giving me thoughts of suicide.

I just want to disappear.
Who would care?
I'm all alone as I am told these heartbreaking words.

No one will ever call me Mom.
I will never have that connection with anyone.
This loss is so profound my cells are crying.

Everything hurts.

So, what matters now?
I have no one to hold me as I cry hysterically when the doctors leave
the room.

These flowers are enough.
I want to throw them on the floor.
to watch the glass shatter.
Breaking into a million little pieces.

I feel like broken glass.
No more value or worth.
A glass vase shattered.
No longer able to carry flowers or water
just as I'm no longer able to carry a child.

No other woman could carry my child either.

Please send help.

I'm broken.

I've just been erased.

Realizing I am no longer a woman.

Endometriosis. Why the fuck are you doing this to me?

My heart feels less female. It's breaking.

Can I go back on lithium and Prozac and be told this is all in my head?

Hope still lived there.

And I wasn't yet erased.

I was still a woman.

Love Letter to My Children

This is a story about love:

To my babies Canyon Joseph and Savannah Alexis,

I am your mother.

There will always be a part of you in me, just as there will always be a part of me in you.

Canyon, I trust you were already waiting for Savannah when I was pregnant with her, because you knew she was going to come to you, not me.

That's why my pregnancy with her became a false pregnancy for so long after the miscarriage. I felt both of you within me all at one moment, and I wasn't ready to let either of you go. Losing you alone was too painful. Imagine now the loss of your sister. It was too painful for my soul to bear.

Enduring this second loss was a ripping apart of my heart that still had not healed.

Canyon, you opened your arms to help welcome Savannah to heaven, didn't you? I can imagine you reaching out for Savannah. I felt that pull. I felt your embrace. I'm glad my mind finally accepted the loss. You helped me with that. I thank you, son.

You both still walk inside my soul, as if your hearts still beat within my womb that no longer exists. I feel your kicks like imaginary knockings at my front door. I want to answer and let you in and never let you go. Instead, I suffered a premature, twisted form of empty nest syndrome almost two decades early.

You are both like twin flames. We are bound with a love so strong, a belonging, a yearning, an "I can't let go." Ever. We are so connected.

I was broken the day I lost you, Canyon. The mirror reflection of me without you was so painful to look at. I cried tears that turned to steel that entered my veins and covered me like armor. I felt like a knight being stabbed and struck with swords, leaving scars and holes without blood to flow through me, because my heart stopped beating.

I will feel this coldness forever, won't I? It's this Tin Man disease I'm at war with every day.

Numbness and cold steel. Painful heartbeats. Each step closer to you is my only solace.

Still, no one could penetrate my heart for love until I knew I was ready for healing. That took years of therapy and tears. I'm still crying, but your love fills me up.

When I was pregnant with Savannah she was with me longer, so losing her felt like a steel trap closing. It didn't mean I loved you less. Please know that, my lovely son.

I look back now, and it was just a mirror image of me looking for you and then looking for Savannah, and I was not ready to face this loss again. A miscarriage at any time is just as painful. I will always look for you both.

Both of you, Savannah and Canyon, will always have a part of me in you and a part of you in me.

I read to you, sang to you, and danced around holding my belly with joy, making sure you felt loved before you drew your first breath. I just didn't know you wouldn't. You were already mine the moment the test said positive. It was a visceral sensation every time you moved. I'm so grateful for those moments.

I imagine you as siblings playing happily in heaven as infants. I will always see you as toddlers. I trust you feel my love as I feel yours. You'll meet me in heaven with our family pets and loved ones who have already joined you. You will begin to grow when I'm with you. I may be wrong, and you are growing now, but please watch over one another until I get there. I find such peace in this.

I see you both on the beaches, and at Sedona with shelves of books, in the moonlight where your grandma lives. When our pup Sullivan looks at me sometimes, I look deeply back into his eyes because I see both of you in them. Do you live in him, or does he live in you? Or does he just have a wishing well in his pupils to show me you are both happy and well? His breathing during sleep sometimes brings you both to mind. It feels like love.

It's hard to be the mother of a child lost in miscarriage. You are never recognized as a mother. You cannot discuss the child(ren) you've lost because people don't understand the love you already share feels as strong as their love for their living children. I'm often asked, "Annie, do you have children?" as if my value depends on that only. You don't get invited to things. Other women make your loss so great without even realizing it.

On Mother's Day I often sit with my head low. I crawl in a ball all day wishing I could celebrate my children, instead of always having to carry this sadness.

Why are we not celebrated on Mother's Day? Can anyone tell me I'm not a mother?

I'm so tired of feeling the cold steel of shame wrapped around me, knowing I am your mother, and you are my children. There needs to be no shame in speaking of you as if you existed. We need to wear it like a banner.

You are and were always loved. You are missed. I talk to you and still sing to you.

You are my children. I will always be proud of that.

There will be a day when we will all be together again. I will glow as I believe you do at night like fireflies.

So, look for me! I'll find you, my Canyon and Savannah.

With the most endearing, motherly love possible,

Your proud Mommy.

Xoxox

I Am a Writer

I am a writer.

I write because I need to explore my heart and soul.

I feel so much excess emotion. I'd overflow if I stopped writing.

I enjoy watching everything pour out onto the paper,

even my tears wetting the page.

My tears have words.

Everything I write has a part of my soul in it.

My heart demands it.

Even in fiction, trace elements of me must remain.

My heart is to me as my paper is to my pen.

I write reviews because I want readers to know
the value of other people's writings.

I truly believe each writing has value, and
there is a reader for everything written.

I am a writer because I'd like something to live on after I die.

There is huge value in that.

The comfort is even larger.

I'd like to be remembered or thought of by someone.

Every word I write is a giving up of a piece of my heart.

The page was just a resting place. until someone reads it.

Then. the reader delivers that piece of my heart back to me.

as they lift the words right back off the page.

Be More Like Superman

*L*ife is often ironic! On March 18, 1999, I saw Christopher Reeve give a motivational speech when I lived in Richmond, Virginia. My employer sent me there so I could be a better manager by learning compassion, empathy, and motivational practices. Other guest speakers were Jackie Joyner-Kersee and Elizabeth Dole.

He moved me to tears with his understanding of "facing the end of life," his trouble breathing, but, most of all, his laughter and the love and jokes he shared with his wife. This couple was the epitome of "To love in sickness and in health."

I reflect upon his talk quite often. I can still remember the palpable love between him and Dana Reeve. He spoke gently, and every few words he had to breathe in a tube, and his wife would have to wipe his mouth. Like Tom always feeding me, taking me to doctors, and getting my medicine.

I cannot express this enough: It is very hard to be fully mobile one day, and then have your body shutting down inch-by-inch and feeling like your being held captive. Christopher Reeve said, "But who else would I want to be stuck with for the rest of my life?" So that is often a mantra of mine when I meditate: *Who else would I want to be stuck with?*

I am well aware that I am not in his situation. But I am well aware of the support needed when you can't do things for yourself. We are all human and want to be loved, respected, included and so much more—just like able-bodied people. It is the human condition. So, just sprinkle kindness wherever you go. You never know whose day you're improving.

Reeve spoke a lot about faith and hope. He had no doubt that this was his path, even his destiny. No regrets. He was at peace with it. At that point in his speech, I began sobbing out loud. I was inconsolable. Looking back, I think it is because of this Stiff Person Syndrome. Ironically, he was preparing me. At the time, I thought my reaction was because I had broken my neck, but I did not become paralyzed.

Because I knew he was dying. We all knew it. I was so happy I could be that close to him before he left this earth. I'm so blessed to have heard his words about being funny still. He spoke of his friend Robin Williams always making him laugh. He said they joked about wheelchairs and everything. It made me realize you really can't be that serious about what's wrong with you. It's okay to laugh sometimes. And trust me, I laugh a lot with the people, who let me talk about what I'm going through or with people going through the same thing as me. Especially with my nurses at the infusion suite. We all laugh hysterically. We call ourselves the "Tuesday Infusion Crew." We think we are the cool ones.

Enjoy everything your body can do while you can. It is tough when you have to count to 3 six times before you finally get the nerve to out of bed to brush your teeth because it is so difficult.

I realized he was more Superman now than he was in his red cape! He taught that whole coliseum how to go out and be better citizens, and he was spreading that message all over the country.

This was what he chose to do at the end of his life.

I wish I could do that. We all choose something. Many of us with disabilities or debilitating terminal illnesses are giving back.

I read that Dana always sang to Christopher. I cried because I always sing to my pups. I've recorded every song, too, just in case. We all want our lives to matter.

That is our greatest hope. I know it's mine.

Be more like Superman.

In honor and memory of Christopher and Dana Reeve.

Lucky in Love

*A*fter the tragedy of 9/11, all I could think about was being near my family, whether it be the family in New York or family in Ireland. So, I visited Ireland, and I realized if I was going to have a job there I was most likely going to be a bartender at a pub which would've been fine. I really enjoy doing that, and those Irish pubs are a lot of fun.

Then I was offered a job in New York City with a company that developed Microsoft software for windows and doors, and other companies like one of the most famous jewelry stores in Manhattan (with designs often worn during the Oscars); the city's biggest Italian food distributor; and a famed fashion house. A lot of different companies utilized their software. I was enamored by everyone in this office when I met them, and I felt like I would be comfortable there.

I decided to take the job in New York. Moving to Ireland was going to have to wait (again). Did that make me sad? Yes, I wanted to live there because so much of my family is there, I adore my family, and Ireland would've been a lovely place to live.

My friend Janelle came down to Virginia to help me move to New York. We got the huge box U-Haul truck. I absolutely cannot believe how much stuff I had. It was ridiculous. I was going to live with my father and step-mother until I found a home of my own. I had to leave my cat Sanka at a vet to be boarded and cared for until I could bring her to New York with me. That devastated me.

I got to New York on December 1 in the evening really late, so we unloaded everything very quickly (thank God I was healthy back then).

The trip to New York was hysterical. Janelle and I got lost in JFK Airport. We were in two separate vehicles, and we were using little CB radios to speak to one another. I was terrified because here I am in a box truck, driving around JFK with no clue how to get out. Janelle and I didn't know what to do with ourselves. It was funny and scary at the same time. We eventually found our way without any hassle from police officers.

Once we unpacked everything, we returned the truck to U-Haul, and I went home and went right to bed. I was completely exhausted, and I had my first day at my new job in the morning.

On the way to work I saw a sign that said "Drive-Thru Coffee Truck." I followed the arrow, and I turned right, then I was on a line with just a few cars. As I was pulling up, I noticed a really good-looking man. He was talking and laughing with everyone. I said to myself, "I'm going to marry that man!"

The girls at my new job must have thought I was crazy, because they said, "Oh, you already got your coffee,"

I said, "Yes, and I got it from the man I know I'm going to marry."

Of course, they laughed at me. Here I had been in New York less than twelve hours, and I was convinced that I'd met the man I was going to marry.

I went back the next day for coffee. And I went back the day after that and the day after that. I did this every workday for a year and a half.

When my girlfriends Crystal and Val came to Times Square for New Year's Eve, I told them that we had to go to the coffee truck in the morning so that they could meet Tom (the man I was going to marry). They also thought I was crazy. But we all went, and they met him. It wasn't just that he was handsome. He was kind, and I loved how he laughed and got along with all of his customers. That says a lot about a man.

I started putting things in my car when I went there with the hope that I could draw his attention. Maybe he'd be curious about why I had fishing gear or the game *Twister* in my backseat. I wanted to illicit conversations beyond my "coffee light and sweet and buttered roll and banana."

Then one day it was freezing outside. He was speaking with a bunch of landscapers, and I saw him take off his gloves and give them to one of the men. When I ordered my coffee I said, "I saw you hand one of those men your gloves. Aren't you going to freeze the rest of your shift?"

Tom said, "He has to work all day, and I'll be off in less than an hour and a half." Well, anyone who knows me knows that a man who would do something like that is a man I could fall in love with. At that moment I started manifesting our relationship. Whatever I had been doing was not working. I needed to take action.

After a year and a half, I didn't know if he had a girlfriend or if he was married. I wrote to the local radio station's morning DJ, Maria from WBLI, and asked her for any advice on how I could find out if he was single without looking crazy. If he wasn't single, I still wanted to be able to come back and get coffee the next day. I was terrified of looking desperate.

Well, Maria read my letter on the radio for people to offer me advice. I somehow missed her email telling me she was going to do this. Many of Tom's customers heard Maria read the letter, and it created a buzz on Long Island. Let's be honest, there are not a lot of drive-through coffee trucks on Long Island that have a man named Tom working there with a woman named Annie, who is a regular customer. I gave away too much for Tom to not realize it was me.

Tom asked me out on a date, and we have been together ever since. That was April 5, 2003, almost twenty years ago. That night we saw *How to Lose a Guy in 10 Days*, and then we ate at Red Lobster. During dinner he announced to me that he was aware of the letter I sent to the radio disc jockey. I was in complete shock! But it worked.

We were married on April 5, 2008, one of the best days of my life. The outdoor wedding took place at the Miller Beach Surf Club, overlooking the

Long Island Sound on a gorgeous spring day. The only hitch was that it was a chilly 50 degrees. My bridal party decided that my dream should still come true and braved the cold. I am grateful that my matron of honor, Kim, and junior bridesmaid, Ciara, and my bridesmaids, Christine, Val, and Amanda all agreed to tough it out. It warmed up enough that some guests went down to the water. We danced and ate, and our honeymoon in Sedona, Arizona, was all expenses paid by the radio station WBLI.

Waiting until I was 38 was worth it! Dreams do come true and mine did when we became Mr. and Mrs. Thomas McDonnell on April 5t, 2008.

Love, like friendship, lasts forever,

I Found My Son

I was getting out of the car and already feeling the dip in the horizon as if my heart had just fallen from my chest to the bottom of the Grand Canyon. I wasn't even near the edge yet, but I could feel it. I could feel where part of my heart lived. It felt like home.

It was here at the very bottom where the water's beautiful waves were like magic fingers carving petroglyphs into the sandstone and mudstone to tell stories to my son. Each ring around the water signifies another year has passed without my son.

Now I know what it means to have your heart walking outside of your body. Because here I am, I'm feeling like my heart is already with my son, whom I named Canyon Joseph. CJ would've been his nickname.

I took Tom's hand and held it tightly, but my ache was so deeply unbearable that when I looked into his eyes and he looked back, I let out a cry from the depths of my soul that I've never heard before.

When I was back in the car, all I could think of was how grateful I was that I had Tom with me to help me do this. He joined me in the front seat, and I couldn't stop the needy, painful cry that was burning in my chest. Tom put his hand on my heart and looked closely at me with a finger wiping away my tears and told me to take deep breaths. So, together we started breathing in and out deeply until I was following his lead. We were finally in sync.

Once I seemed to have calmed down, Tom took my hands and said, "I thought you wanted to come here."

I said, "I did Tom, I do. I'm just so happy that we are here. I know I'm crying hysterically, but it's out of pure happiness. I can't believe this, but I think I have found my son. I know it sounds strange, but I truly believe he's here."

I kissed him on the cheek and opened the door as he opened his and we both got out. We held hands once again as we passed the onlookers and I got closer to the edge. My heart was beating a mile a minute. Everyone was taking pictures of one another and of the landscape with birds flying by. Everyone was so happy and pleased and proud. This was the greatest, grandest place I have ever seen as I believed it would be. Therefore, I had planned to name my son Canyon, after the greatest thing I ever saw that nature built. I wanted my son to have that same strength in his name. His middle name was Joseph, after my brother.

My hands were on the railing, and I was as close to the edge as I could get when suddenly an eagle or hawk swooped in front of me. And he just kept flying by. I felt like he was staring me right in the eyes. It suddenly hit me that this is my Canyon Joseph. So, I start talking to the bird.

I told Tom what I was thinking. I thank God for Tom because he lets me believe what I want to believe. It might be true, it might false, but it is what gets me by through.

This is my son's heaven. I'm so glad it's near Sedona, as it is part of my heaven. I trust I will see Sedona in my afterlife.

We turned around to leave and got in the car and before Tom starts the engine I said, "Thank God I believe in heaven."

A Promise to a Best Friend

Today is the parole hearing. It's been 25 years of Robert Turley's 25-years-to-life sentence for killing her. Everything about this day feels sterile. Robert Turley is in a room, and I am scared to imagine who is in the other rooms around him. He is the scariest man I've ever met. He is in prison for killing my childhood best friend, Jennifer. I survived his trying to get me into the same wooded area she was killed.

In the state of New York, parole board hearings are held every two years. You finally finish one and before you know it you have to start preparing for the next one. You see, each parole hearing requires a letter to the parole board, newspaper articles, social media outreach, petitions that need to be signed, calls to my senator, the district attorney, the homicide squad, and more.

It is exhausting. It is a relentless cry for justice over and over and over again.

I have tried to stop doing it, and I just can't. As the dates get closer I start hearing Jennifer, seeing Jennifer, feeling her presence, and I know I am "Jennifer's voice." This is a job I have now agreed to do for the rest of my life or until he is released from prison. Robert Turley stalked both of us, and we knew that one of us or both of us were going to end up dead. It's hard to explain how you can have the best time with your friends and have the underlying fear of being murdered all the time because someone like this is your neighbor.

What hurts most about Robert Turley is that he was convicted of second-degree murder, but I know that he planned it. Days before her murder, he tried to get me to go with him into the same area where he killed her. There are psychological phases that someone who is planning to kill you goes through. They groom you, swoon you, start trolling, begin flirting, capture, and murder. This is what he did. Step by step. When I called the police they didn't want to talk to me. I was told I was too young when I was trying to get involved in the case. I started having nightmares when I was told I couldn't speak our truth. I felt like I was letting Jennifer down for the second time.

He should have been convicted of murder in the first degree. I wish I could still fight this but I can't. The only power I have is trying to keep him in prison.

I've committed to sending in a letter to each of Turley's parole hearings. I am and will be held captive until the determination of each parole board is made. I know the feeling of waiting with bated breath. It is awful. With each passing day it feels harder to breathe. I am listed as a victim for this crime, so I can get the results earlier than when they are posted online. That is my only sense of relief.

The nightmares start again on my first night home.

I jump as I imagine the gavel hitting the plastic table where the judge, Turley, the lawyers, and I are seated. *You push the seat back and I'm ready to run.*

It became a dark and stormy day where everything began to turn mysterious and creepy even though it was only 10am on the clock. How much could we have accomplished by 10 AM? But it appears some decision has been made already. I am shaking, and I can feel the tiny hairs standing at attention all over my body. There was not one part of my body that did not want to hear everything being said. Only I cannot be there. They ask me to leave the room, and I start screaming bloody murder. I don't understand why I can't be present the moment the decision is made.

As I walk out, the lawyers are called to the table to speak with the leaders of the parole hearing. I'm outside and lightning begins to strike as if it is trying to start little fires around me. The thunderclaps are so loud they scare the monsters from each corner of the building. Jennifer is angry. *Oh please God, let Robert Turley's parole be denied.*

Our monster named Robert Turley looms before me as I walk back in. I look over at him, falling backwards in time to the terrified young girl I was in the 1980s. The neighbor I knew as Bobby. I hated calling him Robert because it gave him a distinction he didn't deserve.

The lights start to flicker. You've got to be kidding me? *This is it*, I think. Bobby's about to get out of Attica Correctional Facility and leave after twenty-five years.

I cannot live in a world where he walks free. It is too much to ask of me.

I wake up.

I was assured he was staying in Attica, NY. I confirmed with The New York State Department of Corrections that his next parole hearing wasn't for another two years.

I was able to breathe again. Tom has a way of calming me down. I am so grateful for this superpower of his.

Has he turned me into a monster? Sometimes, I want to see Bobby injured so badly. I imagine him in agony or wheeled out of prison in a black bag. In my eyes, he deserves this for killing my best friend, but today I'm just satisfied that he's not getting out of prison. Witnessing that would feel like such an accomplishment. If he's ever released, I will never feel safe.

My only solace is that Jennifer was wrapped in nature, by the trees, bushes, grass, and bright blue sky with billowing clouds floating by. I hope she saw them before she left this earth. I bet they sang to her before he covered her with leaves. I hope you had beautiful music and thought of wonderful things. The idea of her suffering hurts so bad I feel like I've been hollowed out.

My hope is that Bobby will die in a concrete building, all dirty and loud and feeling smothered and trapped. I hope he feels like he's choking, the way he took her life by choking her with her belt. I hope he has the same sensation.

I tuck myself into bed. I finally start to drift off to sleep, and my next nightmare begins:

Bobby opens the door to leave the prison and he's running through poison oak, ivy, and nettles. Every plant is stinging and burning him. He is crying out for help, and no one can hear him, no one is answering his cries for help, and no one cares.

Just as it was the day Jennifer died. The leaves of these plants feel so happy for they have finally hurt someone that they feel deserves this pain. He lays flat in a field of grass with his arms and legs outstretched. His light skin bakes in the hot sun all day. Each plant stings and bites choking him. His severe thirst reminds him of Jennifer. He wonders if she felt this way. He prays he will live. He prays to be found.

He realizes Jennifer must have felt the same way, too, with no one to answer her cries.

Was he learning empathy and compassion on this dark and stormy night? Was he having regret?

No. He is too narcissistic. He only thinks of himself. Only thinks of Bobby.

I awaken and still feel his presence here on earth.

I start to prepare for the next parole hearing by making a list of things I need to do. I must be prepared when I must do this all over again.

New York! Why do you make us do these parole hearings every two years? It's too much. It's too often. It's too painful. We, as the survivors, are never away from the crime long enough to begin any sort of healing.

We're like eggs that you continuously crack open and beat.

Can't he just stay there so I can sleep at night?

Thoughts From a Shaman Named Willow Sky

$\mathcal{M}$y shamanism practice has me calling on my Sage Goddesses and leaders for guidance when I'm in need of spiritual assistance. Burning sage or palo santo around my home to rid it of negativity is one of my most powerful practices. Smudging helps usher it right out the front door.

Because I am an empath, I pick up on the negative energy of others. If anyone around me carries it, I smudge my body with sage, too, and feel uplifted. I am reminded of my Shaman given name *Willow Sky* when I am in these moments. I must remember her more.

The Sage Goddesses are always working for those of us who believe in the power of the smudging. What I have learned is that whether it works is up to me. I must believe in its powers because it cannot and will not work on non-believers. It's just like laughter and joy, I can find it in the worst of times because I believe in its power.

Positivity takes work and sometimes the help of a sage healer. Burning the herb helps remind me to center myself, find balance, and seek joy, love, and laughter even in the hardest of times. Allowing someone else to do this for me gives me the opportunity to fully relax, so I prefer when I have assistance.

Even when the positive things in life seem far out of reach, you can seek them and find them:

- I can especially find them during meditation.
- I try to write five things I'm grateful for at the end of the day.
- I have a list of mantras that I like to use. Everyone can find their own mantra.

- I have songs that are my personal theme songs, and when I listen to them, I feel powerful and positive.
- I whisper prayers into stones and bury them outside for the earth to absorb them to be heard.
- I love working with crystals.
- I have an altar.

My beliefs give so much strength to my life. I am grateful I have an open mind, or I wouldn't be sitting here today with all this agony and sickness that I live with and still be able to laugh and be positive.

I don't want to be holding onto the mindset of this cage that I live in. Instead, I grab the key to unlock the cage with my mind, sage, and positive light. This cage will not trap me or hold me back.

I was told by several people to stop saying MY DISEASE. I accept that these diseases are part of me, and I remain positive. If I deny them, I am denying who I am and I won't have the strength to fight them. Who can fight something they can't acknowledge? You must admit a problem before you can fight it. But when it comes to serious diseases, people shut you down. Telling people not to say MY DISEASE is doing a huge injustice to them. I know, because being told to deny what my body was telling me hurt me for years. It kept me down. Now that I am in an "acceptance phase," I am really fighting!

I want to be a bright light in the world, but most of all I want to be a bright light to myself.

Another December

*H*eaven knows I don't need to hear December is supposed to be a month of celebration. I know it is. I just don't know how to get through this month happily. I've been in counseling for years. I have survivor's guilt and complex PTSD that became part of my life when my childhood best friend was murdered.

Some people in my life judge me for still struggling. Aren't they lucky to not have such trauma they need to move past?

Fifteen short years into my life the month of December became full of grief, tragedy, and fear. Anger. So much anger.

Tom will always say, "Here we go again, another one of your Decembers is coming." He asks me to understand it is coming and to be kind to myself. He is speaking of my birthday and that being the day I was almost lured into the woods where Jennifer was killed four days later. It is all wrapped around Christmas. She died carrying Christmas presents. That day she was shopping for my gift and others.

She left the stores where there were bright twinkling lights and beautiful wrapped boxes and fun with Fa-La-La-La-Las playing on the radio in the store. She told the stationary store owner she was having a great day.

My Decembers have no lights or beautiful boxes or music because everything I have is wrapped in sadness. I want to unwrap this sadness and blow it into the wind. I'd like time on this earth without this deep sorrow. My grief takes such a toll on me and those who love me.

I continue to tell Tom, "I'm so sorry. I'm working so hard for my Decembers not to be blue. Feels like the ground is covered in shards of glass, and the bright twinkling lights are all broken, tearing my feet apart as I walk from one place to the other. Only I don't feel it until it's too late."

Unwrapped beautiful boxes sit underneath my Christmas tree on Christmas Day. I hear my wailing as I cry out for Jennifer to come back..

That's all I want for Christmas.

December, you are my sad song.

Move Me

They are the Poets,
Our weaver of words,
Collectors of thoughts.

Putting words to paper,
Dandelion fields become stars in the heavens.

A touch becomes electronic light.

Then, suddenly,

The Words
are whispered
through the wind.

On flights of air
and become the breeze,
that lightly caresses us.

They'll bring us to attention
and even to our knees,
weeping and loving.

They are the Poets.
They fix the broken
and revere the unnoticed.

Make us see the unseen.

They remind you
To look at the stars,
But see them in your hands.

These wordsmiths,
Move mountains,
And hearts and hope.

Even stir souls.

They cross
seas and countries
and continents.
The world.

They move farther
than airplanes and ships.

They are the ones
who will unite us.

~ written in honor of 2021 National Poetry Day
Previously published in *Once Upon Another Time: A Festive Anthology* and winner
Well Done Poetry Award 2023 from "Well Read Magazine."

28

Kaleidoscope of Tears

*L*ately tears flow freely from my eyes. I'm not even actively aware that I'm crying, but tears are falling down my cheeks. My soul knows when to cry, long before it registers with my brain.

I am crying now because I cannot stop thinking about my last breath. I want to make sure I have thought of everything, and I've missed nothing. I have lists all over the place. There is so much pressure in this. I want zero regrets. Remembering all the people I love and making sure they know beyond any doubt is all I need to do. So, I am writing a lot of notes to friends.

I want to make sure I know exactly what I'm going to do when my time is up. At least I'm trying to plan it best as I can. You cannot plan your death, but you can be fully prepared for it. You can certainly do this at any time, but I feel a sense of urgency. I worry about my last thoughts. I want them to be about what I've done that brought me joy, not what I haven't.

If I looked close enough my tears would be a kaleidoscope of color. There is so much in these tears, from love and happiness to grief to pain and loss. I'm missing people already, and I'm still here. I know I'm not seeing many friends again. I cry as people from my life pass through my head in the same way the kaleidoscope changes color schemes. Each new view is an opportunity. It is so beautiful.

I see different people, different hearts, different ethnicities, and religions, and I hear different languages, too. Suddenly, my tears start to have sound. My crying has become audible. I cry realizing how blessed I have been my entire life.

As I try to take deep breaths, to slow my heart and breathing, my heart is begging for relief. Deva Premal is playing on my iPhone; she is so soothing.

I'd like to imagine all I'm dealing with a calm ocean, but it is an angry sea right now from the frustration of not being able to tend to most things alone. I am learning to be more patient. I am so grateful for this. I wish I could take a six-mile run. Meditation soothes my body better now.

I know I see the colors I love. I see the colors my friends love. Each friend is becoming a color. Auras are getting more powerful than they've ever been. I ask for praying hands to be held up in prayer. I see various religions praying for me. I am so grateful.

The tears are starting to burn me now, because those tears in search of a healing have passed. They no longer exist. There is no healing or cure here. There are only goodbyes. My goodbyes are full of beautiful arrays of color. I hope my loved ones know this.

I can only hope that when my friends who choose to mourn me and cry, they will see bright colors and butterflies and rainbows and know that I am free.

A Photographer Once Told Me

A photographer's vision is his paint,
His camera, his paintbrush,
His photo, his Artwork.

One photo is all it takes
For a true-hearted photographer
To begin the life of creating such artwork.

Once the passion has encompassed his soul,
There is no going back.
Everywhere he looks.
Artwork.

There is Artwork within his Artwork.

A sea of sunflowers becomes an ocean of yellow suns.
An old dartboard becomes memories and stories to all who have ever
played and hit bullseye.

A ground covered with petals becomes something we have all dreamed
of walking on in the sunlight.
And a simple rose becomes a sense that is the essence of the frame.

There is always a photograph within a photograph.
Memories, stories, emotions, all trapped in time.

There is such splendor to see through the eyes of another.

This is the photographer's gift
And it is all absolutely marvelous.

30

What Carrie-Lyn Is to Me

(This poem was written as a dedication to be read at my college friend, Carri-Lyn's funeral.)

She will be the sun breaking through the clouds on a rainy day.
And she will be the breeze that wraps around me when I need a hug.
She will be the falling star I will always wish upon.
She will be the whisper of the tide rolling over my feet with a comforting touch.
She will be in the smiles on everyone's faces I see.
She will be in the laughter that makes my stomach hurt.
She will be in the dream I have that has me wake up happy.
She did not leave me or you.
She just stepped away to get the party started on the other side of rainbow bridge.
She is listening to country music, memorizing the words and singing along.
She is dancing with one hand in the air with a huge smile on her face.
She will always be the happiest, most positive person I know.
She will always be with me in my heart.
She will always be the close friend whom I will still call upon every day.
She will now grant the blessings that she always asked me to pray for.
She will always be the light that will never fade.
She will always be C-L.

~ RIP Carrie-Lyn Hobson
(June 21, 1968–July 11, 2011)

Apron Strings

*M*y heart sits on the shelf along with the five positive pregnancy test sticks that I saved. I could never believe I was so lucky!!

Beautiful pastel color apron strings hung everywhere on the shelf. I always imagined myself cooking for you, tying on my apron strings around my waist and neck and pressing play and repeat for our favorite song called "Apron Strings" by Everything but the Girl.

I imagined everything you'd wear would be pink, my little pink lady. There were pink clothes folded neatly in little piles. There were tiny little socks and shoes. So cute! There were handmade hats and sweaters and pants with gorgeous ribbon that matched. There were blankets that were crocheted, knitted, and quilted. I have a love for handmade things...you would've learned that about me.

We planned to bring you home from the hospital in a yellow handmade outfit that I wore home as a newborn. I know it's not pink, but it is the color of dandelions. We will make our wishes upon them playing in the parks, laying in the grass looking up at the sky.

We will probably plant some in the yard. I know they are weeds, but every little girl deserves wishes in her yard.

So many stuffed animals and homemade ragdolls. I wanted anything you touched to be soft and homemade and stitched with love.

On the shelf there was a little rocking chair and a table with songs and stories and poems that I had written for you. It looked just like your bedroom.

There were pictures of your entire family and frames and pictures of your sonogram photos.

I can see your wood building blocks and your doll house.

I will always read you bedtime stories.

I always try to light candles with scents of lavender and baby wash, filling the air reminding me of what you would've smelled like if I were to sniff your hair. Your baby bottle, binky, and bibs and all sorts of little things would be on the shelf, as well.

You must have a puppy of your own, so we would've adopted one of those. I imagine she's running around knocking everything over but laying on your blankets.

I also wonder what you love best about all the things on the shelf,

I know I'm selfish because I always wish it to be me, but I can promise you this, my baby Savannah Alexis, there is going to be a vase of daisies on the little side table next to the rocking chair...when you pull off the little petals you are only to say, "she loves me, she loves me, she loves me." Because no matter what, that's what your mom is doing, she's loving you!! There is no "She loves me not." That will never live between us.

You are on a pedestal in my life. You will never be forgotten. I will hold you and love you when I join you in heaven.

My dearest daughter, my body cries for you like a wild animal in the forest. It is innate and visceral. Do you hear me? If not listen closely.

I love you, my dear, Savvy.

Xoxo

Thoughts of Love

Tree limbs reach above the clouds,

    like babies' arms at birth.

After struggling to become

more than they are now,

    hoping to complete their life's

Puzzle with this one piece

that fits all situations

    like a master key.

A life's journey,

A soul's dream.

Dreaming forward into a future

that never ends.

One that even death won't separate.

Note: Written with ex Jamie Bell and published with permission.
    We took turns each writing a line.

Unconditional Love

*M*y (step)Mom, Carmela, was like a Christmas present dipped in fancy Easter egg colors with a huge, magnificent bow and 4th of July sparklers attached. The kind of gift you get and don't want to open because it's just so beautiful.

Carmela was always a celebration because every day was a holiday to her. She thoroughly enjoyed life. She was a gift of hope, love, and laughter, but mostly security and faith.

Each of her hugs embraced my soul and lifted me up high. I can still feel her in the soft, warm breeze that every once in a while caresses my face. It arrives when I need her most.

I cried in her lap a month before she died and asked what I would do without her. She said, "You love the moon and it's always there watching over you. If you need me, that's where I'll be." She was dying still comforting me, as a mother would.

My (step)Mom was like an island I could swim far away from yet return to as often as I wanted to, especially if I needed rest or care.

Our love existed because of the trust we gave to each other with our whole hearts. It flourished because I felt like I was part of her. I felt like I was always hers. It survives still because she hasn't left me.

My (step)Mom brought out my joy, even when I thought it had been lost forever. She reminded me that I was loved more than those 1,000 cuts and scars that were trying to take my soul. For most of my life she was one of my truest of loves because she knew me most and still loved me.

My (step)Mom always understood me. Her eyes saw only the best in me and forgave me when necessary. I felt wrapped in her love and security like a warm winter scarf on the coldest of days.

My (step)Mom had stunning strength and will-power. When I was burdened or struggling or felt alone, she was there for me. I trust her love and support is traveling across the heavens to me.

When she needed me, caring for her was the least I could do. It was definitely the most personal and honorable responsibility I have ever had. I became her fierce and loyal protector for nine months. Now I realize it was simply her love looking back at me because I was only returning all the love she had ever given me. You would think she had raised me since childhood.

I remember getting her to the bathroom was difficult, so I'd pretend we were dancing all the way there. I would sing, and she would always laugh. We were happy.

I tried to make her dying as special as she made my life. She thanked me a few times, saying I made dying fun. These are some of the most special conversations we shared.

I wasn't sure who I'd be without her. I still wonder.

I keep the copy of a card she wrote to a friend of mine on the refrigerator to remind me how much I was loved by her. He shared it with me while I was grieving her, because he saw my pain was so intense. She asked him to watch over me when she was gone because I "do so much for others and deserve it." She knew I'd be lonely and in need of love without her. She asked Angelo to love me and make sure I was surrounded by love.

Carmela once told me I needed love like people needed air; I was desperately seeking it all the time. No one knew me as she did, and no one ever will.

To be loved by Carmela was warm and encouraging. Never boastful or loud. Never petty or competitive. Her love was never divided.

I hope everyone has this love in their life. Everyone deserves a Carmela. My gratitude is immense. I believe she is now living in the heartbeat of my friends.

God granted me her fierce love, support, devotion, and mama bear protection for almost 20 years.

My (step)Mom Carmela is what unconditional love is and I am so grateful to know exactly what that feels like.

Unconditional Love. The greatest gift of all. It's everything and I do need it as I need air.

Willow Sky Dances

$\mathcal{M}$y roots are so deep and strong the howling winds with their sharp bite can't remove me from my nest. I soak up all the water and earth to sustain me. People walk around me and under me for support; they think I'm beautiful and bring some type of solace to them. I believe most of them are "earthing," which helps the soul to stay grounded as I am. Having their bare feet touch the grass below me is very comforting and brings balance.

The leaves I produce give the sense of weeping as they bow down in reverence as the sun sets. That's why I'm called the willow tree. They hang on strong through my turbulent, painful times in life because I've decided I will live up to my given shaman name - **Willow Sky**.

I trust nothing will break me for I am the storm. My strong, long, graceful branches weep into an arch, creating a round canopy that grazes the ground gently as if they are still "earthing." The willow tree dances and is so stunning.

I am held up by so many ancestors who came before me. They are holding me up back-to-back-to-back-to-back. We are all one. We are a tribe. My trunk is filled with their spirits. Come close and touch me; you'll feel them as you rub your hands along the bark of my trunk or my leaves and branches that hang low in the evening. That power is so profound; it's a visceral experience. You can't see it, but it's there. The spirits. I talk to them.

The dandelions dance under and around me. Come make wishes and watch them come true.

I am named Willow Sky for my strength and wanting to always help others and seeing everyone equally. I was born with hyper-vigilance to need. I dance to the winds coming from the sky, and I always invite others to join me. I can hear the heartbeat from the others who are near me. I want to see myself help heal and comfort others. On a cold day I'd like to offer warmth or if a friend is sad, I'd like to offer a hug.

I'm here. Quietly, willing to listen. Can't you hear the whispers I'm sharing, trying to tell you I'm here for you? *"I'm here, I'm here, and I am not leaving you!"*

I always dreamed of my babies' arms reaching up like my branches for me to pick them up. When the sun rises, my branches and leaves lift up just a little bit. Life was different for me, so my dreams had to change. Now I feel my tree reaching for the gods, goddesses, and you.

I lost Savannah and Canyon to miscarriages, and I believe they're here with me because the love I carry is so profound and sweet it has to come from my children, or at least from the three of us because we are family. Family is supposed to be the biggest love of all.

I was a serial volunteer between hospice, the ambulance, literacy advocacy, dog rescue, and more. I rise as I run away from my problems to help others. I trust I'm still volunteering, just in different ways.

Even when I'm gone, they will study my cells. It is my hope to live on in people because researchers learn something from me. There has to be a reason that I'm dealing with so much illness. I need to give back by helping the warriors born behind me.

I would at least love to see my book on the library shelf and have one person moved when they read it.

Come sit with me. I have plenty of stories to share.

The Message in the Wind Telephone Booth

I walk slowly towards the telephone booth that I've been hearing about for years.

Jennifer, this chat with you has been anticipated for so very long. I've been thinking about the sound of your laugh. I recall the wooden planks in the garage that we pounded with our Irish dancing hard reel shoes. wearing them out to the beat of our favorite Irish music, matching my heartbeat and breath for hours. This memory grows in rhythm with each step as I walk up the hill at the edge of the cliff.

The wind sounds like Irish music, floating down from the heavens and hugging me.

Over the years there's been such a huge hole in my heart, soul, and life. The earth, moon, and sky look and feel different without you. I'm getting closer to the phone, and the air is now getting thicker, making it harder to breathe. Maybe it's my excitement.

My joy has never felt as real as when we were friends. It's been 36 years, 38 days, and 24 minutes since to be exact since you were declared dead.

My thoughts of your last breath riddle my mind. It has always affected me.

I'm told I need to forget the date you died, because it's like a weight around my heart. Occasionally, it's all I think about. I've become obsessed with the time passing by without you here.

I have just a handful of photos to remind me of you and some of the things you loved, like your violin and Irish dancing. We were only young teenagers, so we certainly weren't developing film. You can't imagine the huge regret I carry about this. The regret I carry about so many things with you.

As I walk along the cliff side, there's a hummingbird coming along side with me. I'm admiring the beautiful water below and beyond. Do you see me?

I see beauty more often because thinking of you is no longer dark and murky and painful like a sharp knife wound. I no longer bleed when thoughts of you come to mind. It's only a paper cut sometimes. It's much easier to tend to my paper cuts.

The water is glorious. I wonder *Have you become a mermaid?* There are Irish myths that claim this occurs after death. They are called Selkies to be exact. Are you swimming along the edge of the cliff with me? Are you above me in heaven resting on a cloud? Are you walking alongside me? I often feel you near me. I especially feel you now as I'm walking.

I am going to pick up the phone in the glass booth to tell you a few things. They say it is a one-way conversation, but I sense you'll respond. You always do.

I'm grateful that I believe in heaven so fiercely because I know I'll see you soon.

You could be this very hummingbird that seems to always want to be with me. I seem to be seeing it everywhere. Have you come to take me to heaven? Will this be my last phone call?

The sky is a blue that I can't quite describe, somewhere between turquoise and a bright light blue.

The clouds are billowing, like when we used to lay on the ground and look up at the sky and imagine what each cloud was. Do you remember? "This one's a dog...that one is a lady pushing a cart in the grocery store." Let's play. What do you see in the clouds? I see a clover! I'm definitely getting closer to your voice.

In case I have to wait longer to see you I have a few things I'd like to share when I pick up the phone.

I have to tell you I didn't get married until I was 38! Can you believe it, Jennifer! 38!

First kisses weren't everything, as a matter of fact mine stunk! I wish I was able to have a do over. A lot of things between a man and a woman were often off for me. Never quite right. I think I deserved that.

I'll never get over being the one alive. Being raped twice felt like penance, but not enough.

I often wonder if that's why I've spent my entire life fighting illnesses and now I'm fighting for my life.

I'm losing.

I am losing.

Are you calling me home to you?

Is this survivor's guilt that has my heart beating so slowly that it's not maintaining everything it needs to keep me alive. Is this what death feels like?

I'm so sorry you had to die at only twelve years old. Less than a month shy of your thirteenth birthday.

I want you to know, I'll be looking for you when I get to heaven. Please look for me, too. Maybe you could put up a sign like people do at the airport?

I'm here. It's gorgeous. I open the door and pick up the phone as soon as the door closes.

I close my eyes and decide to listen instead of speak. All I can hear is your laughter. You are happy and say you can't wait to dance with me again as I'm reminded that I'll be able to move properly in heaven. No more walker or shower chair and other aids. I hear my beloved Simon barking. Of course, he is with you! I bet my (step)Mom is in the kitchen cooking!

That's all I need to hear.

Blessings are coming!

I hang up after saying, "I love you more than chocolate itself" and "I'll see you soon, my very best friend."

I leave the Wind Phone Booth with a tinge of sorrow.

As I start walking down the cliff side, I think to myself, "Now...I'm ready to join you in heaven. I'm not in a rush. I am definitely not in a rush. But I'll be ready."

Annie's Note: The Wind Phone Booth is an unconnected telephone booth on the side of a cliff in Ōtsuchi, Iwate Prefecture, Japan, where visitors can hold one-way conversations with deceased loved ones.

Do Not Say Goodbye.

(I read this at my (step)Mom's funeral. The graveside funeral was so special, led by Father Gus Fernando. I told Father Gus we couldn't afford her burial and a church funeral along with the wake. He told me to "kidnap" him and he would perform the funeral at her gravesite. It ended up being a gorgeous day and such a special, intimate funeral)

Each of my mother's footsteps
graced this earth with loving kindness.
Now she will walk in heaven
showering us with the same loving kindness.

Each of my mother's smiles
offered a gift of hope.
Now when each of us prays,
please know she will make sure we
feel that same hope.

Each of my mother's hugs
embraced our souls and lifted us up.
Now when we wrap ourselves in a warm blanket,
or feel the cool caress of a light breeze,
please know that is my mom sending you
one of her great big hugs.

Each of my mother's hands,
held us close to remind us
we are loved and cared for deeply.
Now when you hold someone's hands or just intertwine your own,
please know she is right there beside you still sharing her love and care
for you.

Each of my mother's eyes,
looked at her friends and family and only saw the very best in each of us.

Now her eyes are in the trees, they are in the clouds, and they are in
the waters.
Please find comfort knowing she is
always watching us and wishing us well.
Each of my mother's days
were filled with such strength and willpower.
Now when you feel burdened, are struggling, or even feel alone,
please know my mother will sprinkle only positive energy on you,
so that you can get through that time with the same grace she did
and know you are NEVER ALONE!
So, as we stand here today,
we do not say goodbye to my mother,
because our angel on earth,
has just moved to heaven above.

Rest In Peace Camela Medici-Horsky (10/22/1944 — 4/5/2012)

Everyone Adopts the Right Dog, I Promise!

When a new litter of puppies arrives at the rescue, everyone applies
for the same exact puppy. I think it's just some crazy phenome-
non, but then everyone who doesn't get that particular puppy is just as happy,
if not happier with the one they did adopt and often they'll let us know how
excited they are that they got the different puppy since the one they have in
their home is fitting in so well.

When working on someone's application, you can never tell them that they are guaranteed a particular dog. This is because we don't hold dogs for anyone who has not been 100% approved yet. But I do always share one story with everyone that's quite endearing, so I thought I'd share it with you.

I was running an application on a girl who wanted to adopt a certain dog named Cricket. She was so in love with this dog and her family was so in love with this dog. They had already chosen the dog, and I filled out the application for Cricket right there at the event. Cricket also got a lot of other applications, so I was very clear to this potential adopter that I couldn't guarantee that she'd get to adopt Cricket. I also explained to her that I trust that everybody ends up adopting the right dog for them.

She was not listening. She did not believe a word I said, because Cricket she wanted was the only dog she wanted. As the person running her application, of course I worked diligently to get her approved as quickly as possible so that she could get the dog she is looking to adopt. You create a special bond with the person when you're running their application because they tell you a lot about themselves, and why they think a particular dog would be great for them. Well, one of the things was that she loved Cricket when she saw her at the event was that she was wearing the most adorable little tutu. She was envisioning dressing Cricket up all the time.

After approving her application, I had to call to tell her Cricket had already been adopted. These are the worst phone calls because some people get really upset.

But I asked her to just give me five minutes to tell her about a dog that I believed was her meant to be her dog. She was a little smaller, she was a little older, but she was just as cute, and she also loved getting dressed up and snuggled. So, we put her down for Ramona and she said she was going to come meet her at the next event.

A few days later I received a text from Ramona's new mother. She had told me that Ramona had stolen her heart, and she wouldn't want to be a mommy to any other puppy, along with some photos and videos. These two are attached at the hip already.

And guess what? She adopted the right dog.

I'm glad I told her about Ramona because it wasn't even a dog she was considering. So, it's important that we listen to what the adopter is looking for. Sometimes we can make the perfect match unbeknownst to the person looking for a dog. There's no greater story than these love stories. We know their house is now filled with more love than it was the day before they adopted their new dog. We know a dog has been finally placed in a forever home.

So then we have room to grab another foster to find a home for and the wheels keep turning in rescue because there's always another dog looking for a home.

So, please don't just look for the dog with the perfect spots, or the perfect coloring or the perfect attitude at events. Yours might be the one in the corner. It might be the one with the weird coloring and it might be the one that's barking too much. You just never know.

At One Love Dog Rescue, we recommend that you fill out an application, get approved and then come to an event and meet some dogs. I bet you'll be taking home your forever pet that day!

Rescue a dog, and I promise they are actually rescuing you.

Thoughts on Marriage

Marriage requires a lot of forgiveness
and it requires respecting the other person
even when you disagree with them.
It requires the maturity to put someone else before yourself,
but not so much that you forget who you are as an individual.
Nothing in your life is to take priority over the comfort
and well-being of the person that you've decided to marry.
Marriage requires a listening ear, a shoulder to cry on,
the support to lean on, and love to count on.

Marriage should never be a rivalry.
One of you is never more important than the other.

Marriage is most beautiful in the ugly moments,
because you never waver in your love.

Marriage is caring for your sick spouse,
holding them when they cry,
getting their walker out of the car,
and still thinking they are perfect.

Marriage is holding your spouse's hand
until their very last breath,
singing a song they love
until they close their eyes.

Knowing they were as much for you,
as you were for them.

You are their peace.

Annie's Antics

As I get ready for my online author interview show each day called "Annie's Antics," I realize I am a magician. I perform in this magic show I call "Life Between My Diseases" as well as this interview show.

I always feel like I have an invisible cape on as I fight these rare diseases that try to smuggle into my life. slowly and insidiously squeezing the life out of me.

Each time I get dressed, I feel like a rabbit jumping out of a magician's hat. It's quite a feat. I feel like lightning and fireworks and electric beams all rolled into one. I am always on fire! The pain reminds me that I'm alive.

I require armor and face paint, which I hide behind when on camera. It always feels like Halloween because I must put on so much to cover up the pain I'm carrying. I have this big bag of tricks and my tools always have to be the same brand or they will not work. I can't use mascara that's going to run because I may cry or cover-up that's going to look like cake. There are all other kinds of colorful goodies in there!

My favorite part though is the bag with the lipstick and glosses in it. Because I believe a smile is not a smile unless surrounded by brilliant shine! I love to laugh a lot when I'm on screen. It's pretty much the only place I do laugh these days. It's so real there, too. I love lipstick.

It doesn't matter what clothes I'm wearing.

I'm only in a box on a screen, looking like *The Brady Bunch* intro on the viewer's laptop or their computer or even their cell phone. Thank God my shoulders and below won't matter.

It's easy to fix all of this for a little while. I feel like an actress in a play, acting like I feel well.

I am part of the final magic trick.

I can hardly feel the left side of my body. It feels like I have been cut in half. I'm always tingling and in pain. They say it's all the carbon dioxide in my body that is adding to my pain substantially. I show up to everything a happy-go-lucky gal and ask you to believe this with me, even though I cover it up as I laugh, and I have fun.

I am not willing to show you how sick I truly am. You think you know the whole story, but you don't. I've had TIAs and a stroke. The list is ridiculous.

When I interview authors, my life feels like pure magic. Everything feels like sunshine and dandelions and Queen Anne's lace! I'm so happy talking to authors. It is sublime.

If I were to look out into the audience, I know that the front row would be full of people who know me and are proud of me each and every day. And I know some of my doctors and my physical therapist and my nurses are right behind them cheering me on, as well.

But, just a couple of rows back there are some mean-spirited people who are throwing their candy and popcorn and pamphlets at me because they like to call me a liar, and they bully me because they don't believe me about being in the end stage of my life.

The worst part is they don't even know me. They have never met me. Always appearing in my mind are all those friends who decided they are no longer going to stand by me because I am too emotional. Because my moods change like "presto-chango," and I need a lot of help with things.

With all of my magic powers and my invisible cape I can't stop loving and missing them, even though I know they aren't kind people.

Who gives up on a friend who is suffering? Think about that. Awful people.

I am losing so much functionality. That's what happens when your body stops helping you. I am trapped in my body. I hope you never have to understand the betrayal of your own body.

The hurt I have to deal with when I ask for help, emotionally or physically, and being told "No" is extensive. It sucks watching the friends and family I love walk away so early from my life, slamming the door if they could. It sucks hearing what they say about me behind my back.

I always thought I was a good and kind person. I know I always did my best.

This hocus-pocus disease of mine is at the end stages, and I wish there was another magician running around with the wand that was a simple abracadabra or Alakazamor ponytail I could whip around like the star of *I Dream of Jeannie* that could heal me.

My life has been one of the greatest lives lived, and one of the greatest parts was all the love I did get.

I always say the show must go on, so I'm not giving up.

But I'm definitely resting when I need to.

RIP Stephen Hawking

8 January 1942 – 14 March 2018

"May you rest in peace Stephen Hawking. You deserve this peace. You give me such hope. I will always be honored to have learned from your example. I hope to meet you in the heavens" ~ Annie McDonnell

I trust his energy is now part of this Great Big Universe, out dancing among the Cosmos he admired. Dare I say…if there was a Big Bang somewhere tonight, in another Universe…He definitely had something to do with it.

I admired him for so many reasons, but even more so when I began seeing neurological changes in my body. He made me pay attention to what I could do, not the other way around when I was scared.

He saw beyond his body and what it could no longer do. He allowed nothing to stop him. When he was told he had two years to live in his 60s from ALS, he beat those odds. Big time. Big. Time. He was the body's Big Bang! My fireworks! My inspiration to be more powerful than my nerves allowed.

He lost his ability to walk, so he found a wheelchair he could move on his own.
He lost his voice, and he wanted to still be heard, so he created a way to have a computer speak his words.
He loved learning, teaching, reading, traveling, family, and so much more.
He loved life.
He loved living.
He found meaning in life beyond his disability.
He sought and found his abilities.

He learned as much as he could about our universe, our cosmos...all the way to the Black Hole.

To actually "understand" it and share that information with all of us.

We were all made better and smarter by his presence.

Scholars and patients, students, and caregivers...human beings...me.

Stephen Hawking.

One of the smartest men in our lifetime.

Stephen Hawking.

One of the smartest men in our UNIVERSE .

A man I looked up to. My superhero!

May you rest in peace among the stars!

I know you will shine your light upon us, as you did in life.

Good Love: Thoughts on My Mom in Heaven

When we walk to the edge of all the light we have
and take the step into the darkness of the unknown,
we must believe one of two things will happen —
there will be something solid for us to stand on,
or we will be taught to fly.

~ Patrick Overton

I was my (step)Mother's caregiver for the last nine months of her life. She decided both graciously and heroically that it was time to stop her treatment for breast cancer. I was a volunteer at hospice, so I was well-equipped for end-of-life care with dignity. I was determined that my mom was going to have the best end-of-life experience! Each day was new for us—beautiful, poignant, yet celebratory. She actually thanked me for creating an special time for her. Fun, she called it! Caring for her has been my highest honor. Carmela, my (step)Mom, my Mom since 1991, offered me grace. #TissuesToTheMax

She loved me.

Yesterday was my (step)Mom's 74th Birthday. Although she is in heaven., we are connected. So,this love note is for you, Mom.

October 22, 1944, is such a special day because the world became a better place the day you were born.

October 3, 1997, is such a special day. My world became a better place because you married my dad, and I was able to officially start calling you "Mom." But we knew you were already my mom.

Thanks for all the LOVE you showered me with. I know you are still doing that from heaven. You told me you'd be doing that while sitting on the moon, my favorite place up there.
I will always love you "To the moon and back."
Love, Annie a.k.a Cindy. (Short for Cinderella LOL)
Four years ago...today...my (step)Mom was called to heaven. I will see her again...one day.

Four years ago...I lost one of the most AMAZING women I had the pleasure to know and love.
She loved me so very much; she treated me like her real daughter.

She always told me I was a wonderful daughter. She thinks I spoiled her. Truly…it was the other way around.

My last birthday card from her said that the best thing about me was that was that I chose to call her Mom. I always told her she was the gift!

Our love was one of a kind.

One day when she walked into the house, I was on my hands and knees washing the floor, because I loved to keep things clean for her. She laughed and bestowed my new name on me: Cinderella. She was never the evil stepmother, we just joked about it. After that, she called me Cindy and on all of my cards she wrote DEAR CINDY!

She was such a light in my life. She was an inspiration.

If she was alive today, she'd be bringing me soup and doing anything to make me feel better. She would sit with me, and I'd lay my head on her lap while she stroked my hair, and we watched a movie and talked. She would drop everything on the days I did not feel well. She helped me through and was attentive to all my needs. She was the greatest mom. Very attentive.

She and my dad always needed a call from me so that they'd know I made it home safe from work. She always told me she loved me. She always cared.

I miss her hugs. I miss her stroking my head when I cried. I miss her listening ears. I miss our fun. I miss our laughter. I miss calling out "Mom" and hearing her respond. I miss her telling me to let my hair down. She said it was too pretty to be pulled back in a bun.

She had traditions she shared with all my friends and me, making my life so joyful. The holidays are not the same without her.

I want to follow in my Mom Carmela's footsteps; by being a loving, giving, kind, maternal woman. Even though I don't have children, I can still be there in a maternal and nurturing way for my godchildren, nieces and nephews and other children.

I know she was always proud of me, but I do miss her telling me that. She often did. She knew I was needy for this. I want to keep making her proud.

I miss her telling me to stop wearing my hair up, because she said it looked horrible! She constantly "primped me" when I was leaving her, even if was just a brooch or changing my earrings, etc.

She gave good criticism.
She gave good love.
She gave good advice.
She always gave of herself.

I am grateful she was such a huge part of my life for as long as she was. She is still with me. Yes, I'll be talking to the moon tonight.

So, while today is both my wedding anniversary and the anniversary of her passing, it is a bittersweet day.

Today I celebrate.

Love.

Lots of love.

She taught me a lot about that.

That is her legacy.

Today, I will not cry because my heart is too full of my love for both her and my husband.

Some people never fall in love...I did.

I fell in love with Tom, and I fell in love with my (step)Mom. I fell in love with nieces, nephews, godchildren, friends, and our pets. That is the best way to explain my love for her. She was one of my biggest loves!

She died on our four-year wedding anniversary. I think she managed to choose that day on purpose because my stepmom was all about Love. She knew that I'd have to be sure to do something to celebrate my husband on April 5th each year, so I wouldn't spend the entire day wallowing in the self-pity of losing her, my other soul mate.

Can your stepmother be your soulmate? It did not feel like it at first. When my parents first divorced and my father introduced me to Carmela, I was jealous of her family. She had a daughter, granddaughter, mother, and brother who were over every time I was visiting my father. It drove me crazy. But I soon learned that she was just a big ball of love! Her love was incapable of division. It just expanded.

I gained another family the day my father met my stepMOM.

RIP MOM. I LOVE YOU.

My Body Is My Temple

My body is my temple.
I know I only get one,
This entire life.
It has always kept me safe!
It has always kept me alive!

I broke my neck in a car accident.
I shattered my elbow and broken my feet.

I have had more than thirty surgeries.
I have five rare diseases and others to boot.

I have lost most of my organs' function
Because they became diseased.

I get infusions every week or more,
Just to keep my body going!

Even worse,
I've been raped twice
And I've lost children.

Because of this
I believe I am a Survivor,
Because I know I am a Warrior,

I have the strongest heart.
I have had surgeries to secure this fact!

It still beats with love
And faith and hope.

My soul knows when to cry,
When to give in,

When to rest,
And when enough is enough.

All of me knows how to love with fierce abandon.
I plant that love everywhere,
With each step, word and breath.

I may be overweight.
I may have several scars,
But I must remember
those are my badges,
They are my inner roar!

I may be getting tired.
But it's a result of my story.
And, of that I am proud,
I try not to complain.

I am a survivor.

I love my body!
It is my temple!
It has always kept me safe!
It has always kept me alive!

I wouldn't change a thing!

I truly wouldn't change a thing!

Written in the Stones

*I*t has been so long since I've taken a walk, so I dream of walking my dogs at South Haven Park quite often.

My last thought...A young child makes a wish and blows on a dandelion....as I close my eyes.

It is always during my naps that I imagine these walks, so they feel like quick snapshots in time. Feelings that pass too quickly. The irony is I'm wishing for more time during these dreams. Simon is walking with me and Daphne and Bonnie and Sullivan. My babies. How strange that Simon is with us; he has already gone to heaven.

I feel fully able again. I can use the leash for the dogs, and I can have them run on their own as I chase them and play. I can even catch a ball and throw the ball to play fetch. I am free here; there is no cage binding me to carry this heavy body and what feels like a stagnant life.

But my babies aren't on leashes; we're all running free. Everything about these dreams feel so free and happy. They are the kind of dreams you're having when you don't want to wake up because you know you're dreaming...but this time it feels different. I can't wake up.

Suddenly we're walking through the red rocks of Sedona, Arizona. This place is so magical to me, so of course here it is in my dream. The energy from the stones under my feet feels alive. I can feel the heartbeat of the earth; we are beginning to beat together.

We all enter a special vortex area that I love for its energy. We sit and rest to have some water and a moment of thanks. I have so much to be grateful for. My dogs understand my gratitude better than anyone else. My dogs understand my love better than anyone else. They never doubt it. Something tells me this is why they're with me.

So, as they give love and thanks with their wagging tails and I return it with pats on the head, I give thanks, all this love and thanks swirling up into the air. We're all beginning to feel it. Suddenly, I'm feeling butterflies in my stomach, wait...this doesn't typically happen during my dreams. I need to wake up. But I can't. My eyes won't open.

Could this be my last dream?

As I watch my Daphne and Bonnie and Sullivan go "poof" into thin air like magical dust, my heart begins to bleed, and I cry. Simon knows this and he comes over and puts his head in my lap and his paw in my hands. I start petting him. I don't understand what just happened but I'm still feeling love and gratitude, for Simon reminds me. But none of this makes sense.

I stand up calling their names! "Bonnie! Daphne! Sullivan! Come to Mama!" I feel like my heart is getting lost in sorrow with their disappearance. Simon looks at me as if to tell me to follow him, so I do. Just as we start walking a beach appears on one side of the desert.

This is just as I imagined my heaven to look like. Only we are on the moon.

Simon is running along the water's edge. It looks just like the beach in Shoreham, full of rocks that sit on the sands. I love this beach and I love the red rocks of Sedona...that's why my heaven is split in two. I look back at the red rocks of Sedona because that's where my babies disappeared. Aren't they coming back?

In the stones I see a message, "See you soon Mama." They have gone home.

I realize I am in heaven to stay. I have died. My heart hurts but I realize that I can still feel the earth beating below my feet and that's because so many people love me there. My heart is still beating up here in heaven because so many people love me here, too. I don't think my heart will ever stop beating, for the love I have to give has always been eternal.

I realize my dogs have escorted me to heaven. Of course, they were the ones to bring me here. They have always been my angels!

Simon and I are walking along the beach when I look up and I see my stepmom and my best friend and my grandparents and all the people who have died before me. They are walking towards us. Each of them is holding a rock. For some reason they're handing me these rocks and I don't know why. I'm crying with joy and sorrow all at once, joyful that I'm seeing all my loved ones again that I've missed for so long and sorrowful for leaving the ones I love behind who may choose to mourn me.

Suddenly it dawns on me, this is how I'm going to communicate with those on earth. I will leave them rock messages. I was given these rocks so that I could respond to my babies' messages. I spell out: "Take care of dad, he'll need you more now!"

I know I will see them all of them again in my heaven when it is time. Until then we have rocks to leave each other messages.

Tom is trying to wake me up from my nap. I did not wake up this time.

After burying my body, he begins frantically looking for rocks, and takes the dogs for a walk in the red rocks of Sedona. He has something to tell me.

True Blue

$\mathcal{I}$ have been in the hospital too many times lately, and when I come here, I'm often admitted for many days.

Last night I turned blue because my oxygen dropped below 50. It went below 60 two times. Apparently, I had a very rough night.

My nurse's aide, Valerie, came in to tell me that my oxygen kept dropping all night. She said she was so scared and asked me never to do that to her again. When I saw the look on her face, I knew I was in trouble. Now I'm understanding how close I am to death.

Valerie explained to me that each time they were bringing up my oxygen, I'd wake up very confused. I thought Reagan was president. I was imagining it was my college years. I think that is because my life changed drastically when I broke my neck in a car accident with Tim in 1989. I gave them answers to questions as if it was before the car accident.

I am already grieving my life, yet living happily, cautiously aware that I can stop breathing any evening. This is how a person in the end stages of Stiff Person Syndrome typically dies. We stop breathing, or our heart stops in our sleep. I desperately need sleep, but it feels like sleeping with the enemy.

I am still trying to remain positive. Positive in a way that living would be amazing and death would be, too. I must believe that both have wonderful attributes, or I'd be balled up whining on the couch each day.

I do feel like I'm dying 1,000 small deaths. Alone.

I am trying to deal with it all while loved ones tiptoe around it. Really! They tiptoe around me!

In walks a priest to offer me my Last Rites. Of course, I say yes. So here I am getting my last Sacrament. I didn't think it would be this soon. But I know I don't want to die without it.

He asked how I was feeling physically and emotionally. The first thing I talk to him about are friends and family I lost this year. I think the pain of this year's losses alone could kill me from heartbreak. It is constantly on my mind. Any of my friends can tell you how broken I feel.

I tell him about my texting a certain person (who shall remain nameless) about my turning blue the night before and their response in the text was "Well at least you're where you need to be." I thought they might want to pick up the phone and hear my voice. They didn't. I had to start accepting I was not loved enough by said person. I finally decided to give up.

As I was crying, he told me that I was God's child, and because of my face he could tell I was indeed loved even if I didn't feel like I was. He said, "Excuse me" and left the room.

He came back with a box of tissues. I laughed because I have this thing for books that are so good, they require tissues. It was a simple reminder that I have a cool and awesome life to live.

But, to think Father John was sent here to give me my last Sacrament. Now I know why they ask us what religion we practice. As he gave me my Last Rites, I cried. For two reasons: one, it was scary, and two, I realized how lucky I was to be loved by God. It was unbelievable. As he was doing this, he remembered everything I said to him and repeated it back—praying I could find peace in all I told him. He knew my diagnosis, which surprised me, and he asked for God to give me whatever I needed.

Being in a hospital bed so many times this year made me worry that it might be the last place I lay my head. Alone. This COVID pandemic has stopped the hospitals from allowing visitors.

I just wanted to be home with Tom and our pets.

When the priest left, my roommate, Lily, said "I am so sorry for what you are going through." She was 84 years old, and we got very close during our stay. She was so kind to me. We were together for eleven days.

God sent me someone like Carmela, my (step)Mom. Lily was just like her, and always said what I needed. My (step)Mom was the same way. Comforting, loving, and just kind, in general.

Whether Lily was truly Carmela coming to me on earth didn't matter, it was the fact that I believed it. Because she was who I needed.

If I told her what happened to me the night before, she would've been by my side. COVID be damned, she would've found a way. I still desperately needed someone like her in my life.

But, since I didn't have that, I had to count my blessings and remember I did have her once in my life. Memories of our time together had to be enough.

MY (step)Mom would've showered me with love and hope and hugs if she heard I turned blue.

My (step)Mom cared.

Someone loved me. My (step)Mom was true blue.

Spread Love Everywhere

The dew was still warming in the sunrise as we arrived at the barn on the seven acres of land that was for sale.

The barn itself was decrepit.
It looked like too many lives had lived here and the seller had just given up. As I moved closer, I could smell both birth and death. I was surprised by how similar they smelled.

The walls had chips and the gates of each stable had dings and I knew that the animals that once lived here were just prisoners.

I could hear the cries as I observed each scratch and all the hoof prints. I rubbed my finger down one low to the ground, and I knew a mama had given birth alone crying out for her owner's help. The suffering was intensely palpable, it made my heart ache. I began to cry.

There was no love left here. I felt this each morning walking out. I saw straw here and there but no seed, no food or water bowls of any kind. So much was left behind it's hard to imagine the possibility of these animals living without such pleasures.

These animals had to fend for themselves until they died like the owner of this land. Alone and sad. I was going to make sure this didn't happen again here. Loss hung in the air itself, and I had a chance to repair this land and barn just as my heart needed healing.

I lost my boy Simon a month ago and his love needed to be shared as my life went on without him. I needed a purpose to get up each day or I would turn into an animal trying to claw its way out of this hell in captivity.

My heart needed to feel its beat again. I keep hearing Simon telling me to rescue animals, and I know him, he's not telling me to save just one.

I'd love to heal this land and my heart by setting it up as a rescue/sanctuary. I would name it The Sanctuary of Simon's Heart Rescue where we could help place animals for adoption and hold on to the special ones that are too ill or too old for adoption.

At night I sit and look at the moon and stars knowing Simon, my (step)Mom, Jennifer, and my family who have gone before are looking down and watching over us from that beautiful orb lighting up the sky. It is the kind of bright moon you want to make wishes on.

I look down at the pasture and I see a flood of dandelions. I stand and run through the field, kicking some of the dandelions. I enjoy watching all the seeds flying around me, spreading love and wishes everywhere.

As I ran, I wished for the sanctuary to be filled with love. I said it over and over like a mantra. Then I started calling Simon's name, calling out to my mom and Jennifer. I asked him to come join us, as we rescued animals and showed them the love that they deserve.

They are voiceless. And I'm going to scream loud to rescue more dogs. I felt I had no voice as a child, so I know how these animals feel.

Of course, this is just a dream that I have repeatedly.

I am thankful to remember my sweetdreams. Obviously, I dream about things I would love to have and places I'd like to be and what I want to surround myself with: animals. Our house already is a zoo!

If only I could buy a zoo or a farm and hire people to take care of the pets as I worked in the office and still had time to go love on the animals.

Oh, what a life that would be!

#OperationSimon

S imon was in a cage for almost two years. His time was up until Allyn and Laurel rescued him. They were Simon's heroes that day.

We had a dog-friendly office and when he was walked in, he immediately imprinted on me. Animals pick their human, and he picked me. At least that's how I imagine our story. He was sitting next to my desk and just staring at me, so I took a photo of him. I put it on Facebook and wrote "I'm in love with a dog." I had the sense he was going to be my dog one day. To feel this way was completely outrageous. My bosses were wonderful animal lovers, and no way they were going to give him up. Besides my husband did not want a dog.

After we babysat him for a little while, Simon never left to go back to Allyn and Laurel's house. Tom swears I had a plan, or they had a plan for Simon to stay with us, but we didn't and that's the truth. Ultimately, my dream came true. Simon became our dog.

Seven years later, our house was filled with the most unconditional, amazing love. Then Simon got sick. He developed crazy symptoms out of nowhere. I rushed Simon to the veterinarian. His lethargic state was concerning to me the most and then he started howling like I'd never heard him do. I was terrified for Simon. I was mad my boy was hurting. I couldn't concentrate on anything other than his care.

His vet, Dr. Lou, was shocked to discover he had diabetic ketoacidosis (he does not have diabetes), because just a month prior Dr. Lou had run a full panel of bloodwork before starting a regimen of steroids for his chronic autoimmune Lyme disease. Simon had lost four pounds since then.

My boy's body couldn't handle this last round of steroids. I couldn't leave him for the next 72 hours. The next 48 hours were critical.

They wanted to keep him at the vet office for IV and insulin shots for a few days overnight. I told them that there was no way that my Simon would spend one night in a cage at a place where I was not available to be by his side. I explained that I had been an EMT, and I could take care of his needs. He had been caged long enough in his earlier years. I didn't want him to feel abandoned.

So, they asked me to demonstrate giving him IV and insulin and said, "If you can do it properly, we will gladly let you take him home to continue his medical care there." I passed! We went back home with tons of medicine.

All I could think was thank you Simon for sitting still while I gave you the shots and IV fluids. He was such a good boy. He ate the baby food mix right when I asked him. God bless him, Simon humbled me with the trust he had with me. My love for him couldn't grow any larger. I was trying to take the most exceptional care of him. I truly believed if I did that, he would pull through this crisis.

His ketones were so high they were surprised he wasn't hallucinating yet. Evidently, I had a strong boy! So, we had to go to the vet each morning (or every other) to get his blood sugar tested. He was quite a hit at the veterinarian's office. He got good love there and was taken care of very well. Whatever was wrong with him, they were going to fix it and send us home to continue with IV and insulin.

He was getting a lot of love. All his fur-siblings would come over to love and check on him. I had faith and love to support him. We were doing what needed to be done to get him through this. His vet staff was super kind to him, too.

I asked for prayers to help Simon's little body to manage to beat this. Anyone praying. I was asking for them.

I walked out of the vet office with lots of hope. My worries were dissipating.

After thirty days of this routine, I woke up and saw my boy was sicker than ever, so we shot off to the vet as quickly as we could. I told the staff, "You can't just check his blood sugar. Today he needs to see a vet."

I never imagined that an x-ray would reveal that he was covered in tumors, all brand new over the last thirty days. He didn't have them on his last x-ray. It was the biggest punch in the gut, but I had to love on Simon and tell him how sorry I was that he was suffering. I tried to get him well, and I couldn't.

Tears are dropping on the paper as I write this, Words are beginning to smudge, because I don't want to read them. I don't want them to exist. I want them to disappear. I want my healthy boy back. This all happened too fast. I was not prepared.

I was told to go back home with him for one evening so that his siblings could say goodbye to him. The vet said that they would know. It's amazing how animals sense these things. Tom and I were in shock watching them all sitting around him, licking him, hugging him, and loving him. They loved on us, too. We were about to lose our boy.

I had my last conversation with my boy telling him that since Hurricane Harvey was happening, we would rescue a dog that lost their home due to the hurricane. I told him that we would name the dog Raymond if it was a boy, because we always watched *Everybody Loves Raymond*, or Daphne if it was a girl because we also watched *Frasier* a lot. Simon was full of so much love, and I knew I was going to have to figure out how to share his love with the world, so I told him I would start #OperationSimon by volunteering for a local dog rescue.

The day I took him in to the vet to be sent to heaven I was devastated. His regular vet couldn't even put him down. So, he apologized and sent in a female vet. I don't remember her name. I stopped paying attention the moment Dr. Lou walked out the door. I didn't recognize the woman who came in to give him his last doses of medication that sent him to heaven. I couldn't look at her name tag. I didn't want her to exist. I didn't want her to be doing what she was doing.

I wanted to run off with Simon and run so fast he would somehow heal. I wasn't ready for this, but I never let Simon know or he would be scared.

I started singing to Simon. Looking at him straight in the eyes, I sang my love into his heart. I didn't want him to suffer, and I didn't want him to feel alone or unloved. I was leaning down by Simon's face and holding his paws. I wanted to hold him, hug him, and take him home. I wanted to be doing anything else, but this. This unexpected loss of Simon was too much for my heart to bear. At this moment I understood when mothers said their children were like having their hearts walk outside of their body. I felt like I was dying with him. I may have preferred that.

As he was falling asleep, I was petting him, and I was imagining my fingers were a paintbrush and I was painting him. My mind tricking me into thinking this was all fake. I was seeing all the artwork around the room, and I was thinking what can I do with Simon, so I touched him everywhere to make sure I could paint him later. Pet after pet becoming brushes of paint that could stay with me forever. I could imagine each strand of his hair, its softness, its beautiful shine on a canvas.

Our song was "The Rose." I sang it to him over and over and over again. Once he was gone, I kept singing as if I was extending his breath.

I never imagined he would be gone in thirty days. This was so unexpected. I couldn't accept his death. So, for two weeks I was in bed, until one of my best friends brought over an article for me about why losing a dog is so much harder to accept and understand than losing a human being. It said that dogs are always happy when we come home. They're always happy when they see us. They don't care if we just ignore them for an hour. They don't care if we were just yelling about something. They are always wagging their tails and wanting to love on us. Unlike the humans who are not with us 24/7.

I still sing this song to our new pack of three dogs. Three dogs. It was these three that filled our home with what felt like Simon's love again.

I needed to do something good for Simon and taking these babies in was what I needed to do. I also began volunteering at One Love Dog Rescue. My favorite thing to do was picking up dogs at JFK Airport or in Queens or New Jersey. I loved doing this; it was truly heartwarming and good for my soul.

I later went to a painting event with my high school best friend. She knew it would be good for me to go out and paint Simon. She was right. I felt like he came home that night. This painting hangs in our living room above the TV, so that I always see him.

I began with his nose because he would always bang me with it when he wanted some mama love, like a song or for me to read him a book. Then I moved to the fur that was on his nose because I would pet that a lot as I sang to him. As I was painting this, tears poured out of my eyes and down my cheeks and landed in the painting. My tears mixed with the paint, bringing Simon and I together for eternity.

With each stroke it felt like I was petting Simon. It also felt like I was stroking my pain away. I was hoping Simon felt me in heaven. I realized once the painting was finished, with my tears in the paint.... his shiny fur was back. It was perfect!

I brought the painting of him home and hung it up right away.

Yes, I lost my heart, but I was getting it back one rescue at a time. I loved everything about One Love Dog Rescue. I know Simon is in heaven being my biggest cheerleader. I believe he is proud of me. Anything I could do to help a dog would fill my heart up with love again. #OperationSimon was my mission which began in September 2017.

Part of the proceeds from this book will be donated to One Love Dog Rescue. This work will continue even after I've gone to heaven.

47

Welcome to My New Podcast

Get Over that Grief with Make-Up and Dogs

The delivery of the new "You Will Stop Crying" make-up set finally arrived from "Grief Stricken, LLC!" I was so excited until I saw it is not waterproof! Why was there so much buzz about this? I was hearing nothing but great things about all the products, especially the cream to powder concealer and mascara.

But I look like a raccoon when I use it and there's a thick black line that runs down my face on both cheeks. It is completely embarrassing. You see, I cry often during these podcasts.

But, when I think about it, I realize tears should be dark, so that people can see your pain. We all spend so much time ignoring or being embarrassed by it. We'd rather walk around and act like it doesn't exist. Yet I'm sad; I'm carrying grief. I wish waterproof mascara would run because my tears need to be seen. I need witnesses. I need help.

Speaking of dark, I also love dark eyeshadows. They may as well be called Cemetery Black, Gray Ghost, and Killer Green. I'm not one for bright and happy colors anymore. I'm still wallowing in my grief. These dark colors suit me.

I always have tissues with me because that's how often I have been crying. I'm at the point where I should invest in the company that makes the Kleenex tissues, because they are the ones I like to use best.

My doctor said I should have a cry fest each week and cry as loud as I must. I'm not to wear makeup when I do this. She believes that eventually I will finish my need to cry. I look forward to that day.

My dogs, especially Sullivan, snuggle me when I'm crying, and Bonnie lays her head on me to hug me and bring me comfort. All three of my dogs are amazing at helping me with my pain, both physical and emotional. Daphne is my protector.

I have dry eyes and I needed tear plugs. How does someone who cries as much as I do these days have dry eyes?

I believe that there's the possibility that I'm just all cried out. My body is confused, but my soul is just as out of alignment. My body is in so much pain it will never know that my grief may finally have ended. I might live with this for all times.

I like to think of my tears as love. Love pouring out of my soul because I always say grief is love turned inside out. I just have so much love for those who have gone to heaven before me.

The worst is the grief I carry for my friends and family who decided not to love me anymore. Their "death" is harder to deal with because they're still here. They've decided I'm not here. I'm not in their life. I do not exist. How you give up on your family and loved ones is something I will never understand. But now I am the one taking my power back by not allowing them access to my love. When people can remove children from the love they are getting, they aren't worthy of much of anything.

I should suggest they send me the "I'm So Blue" make-up set with colors like "I Can't Get Over Losing Your Love" or "Please Love Me Again" or "I Miss You (Dear Person Who Shall Remain Nameless)." History is just repeating itself generation after generation.

I really should feel sad for the ones who throw me away. I love fiercely.

Well, folks, if you need waterproof mascara like me, I don't recommend "You Will Stop Crying" because it only works if you don't cry or go ahead and grab it if you want your tears to show and remember Kleenex is like a hug! It is the best gift for a grieving friend along with just listening when they need to talk.

Join me next week for the "I Feel Lonely" lipstick set that puts a smile on your face every time you put it on. I hear it is amazing.

How do you think I'll smile on through this?

Thank you for joining me and I'll see you next week with hopefully a happier tale to tell here on *Get Over That Grief with Make-Up and Dogs*!

Note from our sponsor: Dogs are always available for adoption at One Love Dog Rescue. I promise they will put a smile on your face and give you unconditional love for their lifetime. They may even dry your tears as you move through your grief. Just email adopt@OneLoveDogRescue.org for an application and information.

48

Safety Instructions for Annie

*F*riends and family! ALERT!

Read these instructions on how to operate best when with Annie now that she is in the end stages of Stiff Person Syndrome. This is the end of her life. The last quarter.

Since you have part ownership of Annie's heart, please know that it's best to follow these instructions to the best of your ability if you want to remain in her life. It's imperative. She is struggling, even if you can't tell.

You say she looks good. Trust me, she is not. But she is trying to remain positive and fight. She needs you more than you can imagine.

DO be gentle for she is grieving the loss of functionality and is in pain both physically and emotionally each day. She will break if not taken care of properly. We don't want her balled up in the corner of the basement floor not functioning at all.

PLEASE refer to these instructions if you see Annie agitated or you don't understand something about her. For instance, PLEASE NOTE: Annie will cancel plans to get together, even at the last minute, and she will say no to a lot of invitations. Please know it has nothing to do with you. She wants to be everything for you. We promise. The fun, pretty, skinny Annie is still in there. She wants to be able to be everything to you.

You will need to HEED ALL WARNINGS necessary when having chosen to remain in a relationship with Annie. Disabling illnesses take so much energy out on both parties. It is like Annie's electrical cord has short-circuited and she no longer functions at full power. She understands that it isn't easy for you. It is important that you understand this will not be easy to learn. You must be patient. Annie is also having a tough time understanding everything. She wants to be able to be everything to you.

DO NOT bring Annie too close to the water without a safety vest; she could drown. She is no longer able to swim or even keep herself safe in the water. Make sure there is always a lifeguard present. All swimming safety rules should be followed. Puddles are even dangerous for her. She is often slipping and falling. Annie does like to be in the pool, so refer to Annie's water safety manual for those specific instructions. She knows you like to go to the beach and the pool, too. Annie still wants to have fun. She wants to be able to be everything to you.

DO NOT take Annie out without her walker and wheelchair. You never know which one you will need. Preparedness is key when are you are going out with Annie. DO NOT ask if she needs the walker. She will always need it. PLEASE don't make her feel shame. She already does.

DO NOT expect Annie to be able to entertain you when you visit her. To the person who couldn't understand visits with a child and staying at her home is no longer possible: You are selfish. More narcissistic, really!

It is best if you bring things to snack on and drink or tell her what you need and be able to get it yourself out of the kitchen, because she cannot take care of things like this anymore. This is so hard because she wants to be able to be everything to you. HELP HER STILL BE THE FUN HOSTESS.

DO NOT throw in the towel and give up on Annie. It's so easy for Annie to feel defeated and even embarrassed by these needs each day. If you do them with a sense of ease, Annie will be more apt to leave the house to be with you. This would be so good for her overall care. She tends to be a hermit because she doesn't want people to see her this way. She wants to be able to be everything to you.

PROTECT Annie from being walked on and hurt by others. Especially when people she loves keep walking out of her life. Help hold her up. Be there to support her and love her EXACTLY as she is. Because she really does want to be everything to you.

UNDERSTAND that Annie is going to have bad days. She is going to be emotional, and she may even be cranky. (Wouldn't you be if you were in the end stages of your life?) Don't give up on her.

ONLY USE the proper tools she is given to help her. She is fitted for a lot of things, and she knows how to use them. For example, she has a sock aid, she has a leg lift to help her get in and out of the car. She has a shower chair and bars in the bathroom and even private things that she must use. And of course, the walker and wheelchair. If she is out in public, make sure she uses the handicap bathroom. She will not work properly if she doesn't have these items.

Be sure to UNPLUG her CPAP, parrafin and TENS machine during lightning storms. Refer all servicing to South Shore neurology or Catholic Home Care when necessary.

CALL 911 if Annie acts strange in any way physically. She has a blood pressure cuff, EKG, and pulse ox tool to check her vitals.

Warning: to reduce the risk of hurting Annie's heart and soul PLEASE be patient and kind. PLEASE offer her grace as she figures out how to manage and see herself through the end stage of her Stiff Person Syndrome. The ALERT at the beginning with the exclamation points is there because these tools are needed to sustain a healthy relationship with Annie. She doesn't want to lose you and she doesn't want to stop loving herself...which is very easy to do right now.

She wants to be everything to you. Annie always tried to be one of the nicest people to you, but being sick is causing her to grieve and hurt so Annie can't GIVE as she used to.

Maybe you can be everything to her right now!

Call 1-800-LUV-ANIE if you need to speak with a counselor who can help you navigate being in a relationship with Annie as she is in the last stage of her life. The call is FREE. We know it's difficult.

Returns are not accepted. Annie wants to fix anything that is broken. She doesn't believe in broken relationships. Once she loves someone, she doesn't stop. She wants to be able to be everything to you, even to those who already walked away. Maybe one day you will think of something nice about her.

These safety instructions apply to so many other people. Maybe you have a sick or disabled person is in your life? Please consider these safety instructions when in relationship with them.

Love Walked In

Ode to my friend Lindsey and her husband married 2022

Love walked in and grabbed hold of two hearts
To make them one.
Only they were always walking towards one another.
They just never knew it.

Their lives were already intertwined and aligned for this special day.
I absolutely trust they were chosen for one another at birth.
All soulmates are.

Their entire lives have been their wedding march.
What you'll witness today is simply their final steps

Towards each other in full mind, body, and soul.
Ready to vow to love, honor and cherish one another, always.

They were led to share their love with you, too.

You will watch them as they meet today
And hold hands, exchange vows and rings
And become exactly who they were meant to be.

Today you'll watch their souls being fully realized.
Today they are saying officially "I am yours and you are mine."
To each other and all of you.

This extraordinarily beautiful couple,
Will go forth from here as one,
Raising their pups Koda and Kevin together
May nothing divide them.

Each step they all take now
Will always be beside one another
May they never walk alone again.
For two people can be married and apart and still always walk together,
Because that is where their hearts find their beats.

They were led to walk beside one another.

They will count on one another
Depend on one another
And love one another today and always.

May their love grow deeper with each passing year.

When true love meets
And they stand at an altar to exchange vows
Magic and electric sparks of light
Begin to lead their way
In love and prayer and blessings.

They'll even leave colorful beauty in their wake.

Please watch them today and always,
Bear witness to their love and life
Today and always.

Support them when they need it.
And be there even when they don't.

Love walked in
And grabbed told of two hearts,
To make them family,

Holding hands and hearts and dog leashes, too.

My Emotional Toolbox

*M*y grief has been with me for years, grief for many different things, from the loss of a loved one, the loss of a pet, or the loss of the use of my full body.

It has been suggested to me that I reflect before I move onto the task for the day, maybe even before any task to have more gentle transitions into anything.

Befriend my nervous system. Deep breathing practices throughout the day to make sure I'm present in the moment.

Sighing every once in a while, because this could help my vagus nerve reset. My vagus nerve does not work at all, so I don't know that it resets, but sighing does help for sure, so I enjoy taking deep sighs.

It's also been suggested to me to put a hand or both over my heart, possibly move one of those hands onto my forehead and one onto the back of my head as I'm taking the sighs. These are sounds that come out of me purposefully, so there seems to be some type of electric current that rides with them with a powerful intention of peace.

Distance reiki has been such a powerful tool. I get it mostly from my ZTA sister Cathlyn, and she truly empowers me. My friend, Donnie has a friend named Daniel who reaches out to me sometimes, too. I love reiki and feel its love and energy.

Tapping is something that I learned from Kerry Schafer, and I definitely see certain changes in myself as I am doing so. That has certainly taught me to relax rather quickly.

Sometimes I have to change rooms, or I'll go out into nature, to my backyard or on my porch. Breathing in the fresh air is amazing. If I have someone who can take me somewhere like the beach even if I can't get onto the sand, I can still feel the air coming off the water. That is by far one of the most soothing and healing things I can ever do for myself. I miss being able to jump in the car and take myself independently. I don't do anything alone anymore if it's outside of the house and inside of the house I'm often lonely. It's very confusing for me so I can imagine how it's confusing for my soul.

Stretch. Stretch my body. If I'm not feeling well, I can even stretch laying down. I especially love to stretch my legs with a strap wrapped around my foot or on the big yoga ball. I always feel amazing after a good stretch. I used to absolutely love yoga, so I do try to get into yoga poses. I had a physical therapist named Joanie, and she truly made me feel like a warrior. She was my hero for a year. Each time I saw her I felt like a better person. She gave me strength in her belief in me.

My friends Doris and Joel are so similar to my friend and ZTA sister Denise with their healing and spiritual beliefs. I am so blessed to have them in my life because they have taught me their tools for moving into a more relaxed and authentic state of being myself. Even when I feel paralyzed from the floor in any room, I can find myself and center my soul.

Walking in the labyrinth or chanting is something I always enjoyed doing. Doris and Joel filled me with their wonderment of exploring earth medicine. I became a shaman because Doris told me one time that she thought I was already a shaman, I just didn't know it yet. I was already practicing earth medicine on my own. Learning the medicine wheel, I became a shaman named Willow Sky. I find power in this.

Having my own altar at home with candles and crystals and vibhuti to put on my body and my shaman medicine bag has made a huge difference in my life. I also love earth painting.

Denise runs what she calls a "Soul Shack" for me. To watch Denise have such a deep understanding of her soul and what it needs teaches me a lot, because she has overcome so much. It's kind of like I must believe if she can do it, I most certainly can because she's been through so much, too. She learned to work with crystals and sage in prayer and oracle decks and chakra clearing and so much more. She has taught me everything in her toolbox.

My toolbox overflows with things to help myself if I'm stuck. And that is a huge problem in my life...getting stuck.

Everything she's taught me is big on breathing and getting adequate rest and drinking water throughout the day.

They've each passed their tools onto me. They all feel like they put their footprints alongside of mine. They are true friends, and there's so much love in that.

One of my favorites is listening to rooted frequency music. I had never heard of this until Denise introduced me to it. The same goes with moving my chakras to get my juices flowing whether it be in the morning or at night. Sometimes I slow them down at night and I speed them up in the morning. It's amazing how these frequency tunes change my day.

My toolbox for self-care and self-love is full of so many different things. These are just the ideas that were given to me by friends of mine who have added so much more meaning to my life and the understanding of how I can control my body itself. I believe that's why my fight is so strong.

I can most certainly never thank any of them enough.

My gratitude is endless.

My Soul Guru ~ Denise

Meeting Denise in this sacred space has been one of my life's greatest joys and gifts.

I came to her with both physical and emotional stressors. My body was extremely labored on a daily basis. I was feeling so hopeless.

Denise lightens my load. She helps me unwrap my body's potential for healing. She helps me believe it could be true.

Denise does this by using the many modalities that she either specializes in or has enough knowledge in that she's happy to share what she knows. We have worked with everything from visualizations to crystals to chakra work to listening to restorative music and reciting mantras to working with a mala, music bowls and sage!

Denise even hones in on readings of cards like no one I know.

Denise honors so many traditions with grace and dignity. She has so much respect for various cultures that her knowledge is vast and wide.

I am so much more myself since we began working together. When my disease hit full force, I didn't know it was possible.

Her energy work, especially healing or grounding, is beyond powerful.

She is helping me unlock my potential to live. At least believe in it.

Denise is a force. A force coming out of love.

My friend, my ZTA sister, my soul guru.

Chasing Maps

*N*ow, I follow him by chasing maps.

Today I received a message from the guidance office at Wyoming Correctional Facility in New York, where Robert Turley is incarcerated. He is up for parole, again. Our map is long and winding.

He is still serving his 25 years to life prison sentence for sexually assaulting and murdering my best friend, Jennifer Goff when she was 12 years old.

This is the 36th year he has been incarcerated and nothing has changed. Everything still feels the same. I still feel like that scared, angry, defenseless, ignored little girl. He still claims his innocence. We spend too much time at this crossroad.

I am asked to write a victim impact statement letter to the parole board, so today I hope to be heard.

Two months ago, he was moved from Attica maximum-security prison to Wyoming a medium-security prison in Wyoming. I was a wreck. I wanted the map to end at Attica. I felt safe having him there.

I immediately called his guidance counselor to inquire about the reasoning behind this move. I had so much fear that it meant they were ready to release him. I was told it was because he had been in prison long enough, and he earned the right to move to a medium-security prison.

Jennifer didn't earn the right to step down from heaven and talk to me over dinner. It just feels wrong for him to get this right.

I have often been nervous that he was one step closer to getting out of prison. It was these parole hearings. Every two years! Like an unwanted guest at the front door that I had to entertain. A big stick pin on my life's map. It is too much to offer him every two years.

I have spent 36 years following Robert Turley all over the state of New York from Attica prison to Green Meadow in Green Haven back-and-forth between those two for years. Originally, he was at Coxsackie prison right after Sing-Sing, where I think everybody starts. The fact that we didn't have access to Google for years made me wonder how I managed to keep up with him years ago. I became his stalker.

Right away I became obsessed with knowing where he was. I had to know where he was so I could believe he couldn't come after me.

Even though he was in prison, I would look up how many hours away these prisons were by car. If there was an escape from the prison he was in, I would be on pins and needles until I knew the name of the inmates who escaped. My map of the state of New York showed prisons instead of national parks and colleges and all the other beautiful places. Too many criminals here.

I realize now that all my mapping just kept me living in a prison, didn't it?

When you move lower down on the map, you'll see Long Island. That is where he stalked us in Nesconset and murdered her. The trial was held in Suffolk County, and his original intake was at Riverhead Jail. I include her funeral in St. James at St. Phillips and James where she went to school and her burial in Stony Brook. I still decorate the tree at her grave site each year for Christmas.

My map always leads me back to all the maps Jennifer and I drew in the dirt with sticks while playing games in the woods with all the neighbor kids. You know, the kind of games you played when you were still innocent! Before your best friend was killed, and your innocence leaves your soul, and all of your friends disappear.

After her murder those maps in dirt just turned to dust, and I would never see a map made by children again. I would never play in the woods again. Fear was winning.

My mind became an ever-changing road map tracking him through the prison system. From the very second I found out she was dead, I lost my childhood. Our neighborhood friends all stopped talking. We lost one another. We were all in prison. Just without bars, locks, and keys.

When I was told Jennifer was dead, I felt every single cell within my body being churned and changed, like the inside of a clock freezing me in time with the turn of a key. I heard it. I felt it. The pain was so intense I couldn't speak, cry, or move.

My life's course was being set for a different destiny.

My innocence was stolen went with Jennifer's life.

I then thought of things even adults shouldn't be forced to worry about. It was awful. No one should feel this. It burned. It burned some places in my body so much it felt hollowed out. My heart immediately hollowed out. I couldn't feel it. Numbness everywhere.

It was like an electric zap of light that commanded: "Now, you have responsibilities to keep Jennifer's killer in jail. You know who he is. Call the police. Make sure no one forgets her, and by God...you must learn to live without her. Without her and all the dreams you shared."

The map of my body was changed forever. If I had a tattoo of this, you'd cry looking at me, because of the pain it would convey. I called the police, but I was too young for too many things. It was unfair because I immediately felt like an adult with adult responsibilities.

Thirty-six years later I feel the exact opposite. I feel younger and in sheer agony.

It makes complete sense that my nerve fibers are gone, so I feel every single bit of pain intensely. I have no reflexes because my nerves are just shot. They have stopped communicating with one another. Shock will do that to you. I can't stand longer than two minutes without my body starting to shake like crazy because my muscles just cannot stand it. I don't even make antibodies.

The Annie who was once whole and healthy in mind and body also died on December 9, 1985, at approximately 3pm EST. An invisible force hit me so hard my inner road maps were destroyed, leaving a burning map on the outside of my skin. This would be my new roadmap for life.

My chasing Turley's prisons feels like chasing our innocence. I was hoping to rewind time. It never worked.

I'll always be chasing that map of me in my dreams before Jennifer died. It was beautiful. We were beautiful. She was everything beautiful.

As with all old maps, it's been crumpled up and thrown away.

It's lost. It's gone.

It's an antique.

I need to work with this new map that I hate.

As life goes on, I work hard to make this one colorful and bright. I need to live a little longer before meeting her again in heaven for an Irish dance or some gossip about boys. I need to find happiness again.

I think Jennifer is proud of me for helping keep that man in prison. I will chase maps for the rest of my life. This has been my job as Jennifer's best friend forever.

He stalked us. Now I am stalking him.

Note from author 8/29/2021: Robert Turley's parole has been denied. August 2023, we will do this all over again.

The Clover's Fourth Leaf...Ode to Momsie

To be loved by you is comforting, warm and safe.

I realize over and over again this is how a mother should make her child feel. Since 2012 I have been without my mom, and Carmela or God gave me you. There is no age cutoff to needing or wanting your mom.

Carmela always understood me and my losses and my fears and my traumas and my weaknesses and loved me regardless of myself. She saw only goodness in me and wouldn't let anyone hurt me. She was like a lion protecting me, much like you!

I always wanted to do better and be better. To be someone to make her proud.

Imagine that for one moment.

You have to be that loved to give that kind of love. You are my source.

I love you so much. You are beautiful. You are strong and you are an inspiration.

You are magical!

You see this same beauty in so many people,

Because that is your truest essence.

Everything you see is through eyes of love.

You catch love in your photographs.

You don't even know half of the people loving you.

But you are spreading love like seeds thrown out of a farmer's hand…Blowing in the wind…Dancing to moonlight and raindrops and sunshine, before even growing roots and sprouting.

Before you see the love, there it is. Reaching for the skies above.

I saw it immediately. I felt a belonging to you. Somehow, some way. A calling? A message? My mom asking me to trust someone? A tap on my shoulder?

I just know I am so grateful to be as close to you as I am.

To know your true love has been heaven sent.

To know how you see the world teaches me and my heart and my mind how to see its beauty more clearly.

I hope you realize how loved you are.

You are a calling to see so much more in life. To open my senses wider, to really look.

Please don't ever doubt yourself. Please don't ever think your writing or your stories aren't as powerful or as important as somebody else's just because they have more stories written and published.

Seeing beauty and people, places, and things as you do is a gift and sharing it with the world is absolutely priceless.

If God gave me a mom, I'd certainly ask for you over and over again.

Because it's the love I have for you that shines even brighter inside my heart. Sometimes when talking about you to others I feel like I glow. I feel like my heart beams bright lights and salsa music.

The pride I have when I speak of you is like a three-leaf clover sprouting its fourth leaf.

That's what you are. You're my fourth leaf. You're my lucky charm. You're that rare find. The clover people collect.

You will always be an ocean of sunflowers, lavender, and light.

Because I always think of you.

You are my chosen mom, the one that has chosen me right back.

String Theory

We are always tethered
To those who love us.

My pets, Tom, and I are all
part of the same string tying us together,
making us family.
The family that will not ever break
For there is a ball for each soul living
within my present family
and the line combining us is Tom.

He cares for each of us.
Wherever or however this moves,
we are never separated.
This string could be held as I pray to represent the McDonnell Clan.

This was also chosen for its various colors
Reminding me of the pride rainbow
that our family knows, loves, and celebrates.

The shredding on the string represents
all of the times certain people in my family
have banned me from their lives, over and over again.

I've been made stronger by those fragments
because it is more beautiful and held
together by my immediate family.

But I stay away from the shreds.
They don't share their love.

I am stronger for knowing
my true loves on this string.

Like The McDonnell Clan, who have
never broken away
and abandoned me.

55

An Annie without a Jennifer

I entered my guidance counselor's office
knowing they were going to tell me
something I didn't want to hear.

The room became stifling hot,
my body having shocks that hurt.
The warning signs were flashing
through each of my cells.

The hairs on my arm knew.
The entire muscle of my heart
jumping outside of my body
frantically knew, too.

My body was telling me to leave

I didn't listen.
I was cemented in this one spot.
I couldn't speak at all.

As she spoke, I felt each cell
hollow out inside of me.
They were all banging into
one another. Shifting.

I was emptying.
So much sorrow.

Screaming the unacceptable
cry of denial!
Falling into a hollow chair
tremendously uncomfortable!

My body was absorbing
every detail my ears were hearing.
But, my heart.

My heart obviously did not want
to be part of me.

Not for this.
I wanted to run as far away as I could
to catch all of the happiness and love
I was losing.

My veins were being drained of life.
Or was I just wishing for this?

The words not only broke
my soul in two, but caused
an insidious painful scream
that still resonates today.

38 years and I'm still
looking for you, Jennifer.
Or someone like you.
Even if only in my dreams.

I can't find anyone like you.

This painful, soulful ache
in each cell still reminds me
that this was my first taste
of profound trauma.

I will never be the same.

So much guilt
pouring over me
like a waterfall,
only they were tears.

Tears falling
down my face
like a monsoon.

Jennifer Lee Goff. My BFF.
I realized you were my air,
my light and all things immensely
dazzling in my life.

I loved you.
Too late to tell you all of this.
Shaking in disbelief.

That day I was told you
you were killed,
I became an Annie
without a Jennifer.

I split in half.
I made no sense for years.
It is because I am only
half of myself.

I still get lost in my misery.

56

Iron Will and Strong Constitution!

I've turned the page to my last chapter. My cardiologist called it in like an item on a menu with a side of fries. I am going to go into hospice care.

A MOLST is getting filled out, because he believes I'll be in heaven within the month. It's hard to swallow this.

I'll find peace in this.

I am a fighter, though, so this doesn't mean I'm giving up. I'm not giving in. What it does mean is that I'll be receiving the care I need each and every day in my home. I won't to have to go to the hospital each time my chest hurts or I get dizzy or fall and spend the night or even a week there. Now, I get to stay home with Tom, my dogs, and cats. They are my comfort, my loves, my family. The doctors and nurses will come to me.

I'll find peace in this.

When I was caring for my (step)Mom and she was placed in hospice, she told me I made dying fun, so I'm going to be sure I do the same for me! I plan to have a beautiful ending journey. There can be beauty and honor in all of this sadness. I can remember I've been given a gift! The gift of time to say goodbye. Not everyone gets that. I feel blessed.

I'll find peace in this.

This decision for hospice was made after my cardiologist ran a critical care assessment (CCA) that reported I'd been critically ill for several years. I've known that, because I've felt my body shutting down, and my systems had not been communicating with one another. The doctor was amazed that I was there before him! He says I must have an iron will and strong constitution! Tears rolled down my face.

I cried because I knew I'd been pushing my life uphill for years.

I cried because now I was heard. I cried because they heard me too late. Again.

Just like when I had endometriosis.

I epically failed the CCA, and I finally had proof of all I'd been saying for years in black and white! Thirty-six pages long...36 pages of dysfunction. My shock was so profound, I was rendered speechless.

I still wanted to fight.

But there was a beautiful moment of grace that washed over me. A moment where I gave myself permission to say, *It's okay to just be. It's okay to give in. It's okay to rest.*

I'll find peace in this.

Dr. Varma texted the head of hospice right then to make our appointment to enroll me.

He said I was to live each day as if it were my last.

Now, he says that each time we speak, because we still don't know when my last day here on earth will come.

I know we could all die tomorrow. I wish people would not say this to me because what I hear is: "I don't care that you are carrying around a MOLST and know you are facing death." Maybe "Are you scared?" would be kinder. Nothing is worse than feeling terrified and having your loved ones diminish your feelings.

The difference is, I'm absolutely facing death head on. I am actively planning my death. First thing I must do is find where I will be donating my body to science. I'm in hospice care. I've filled out my MOLST (the doctor and I sign this to implement ALL of my end of life care. This is only for people the doctors believe will be gone within a month. This feels very, very REAL to me. Death is knocking, and I'm about to answer.

I'll find peace in this.

You see, surrendering to God's will is allowing his grace to soothe me through this process. In acknowledgement, I am living as if it's the end, but I still surround myself with crystals and prayers and any other goodness I can wrap myself with to ask for a miracle or more time on earth. It's a fine line.

I've been given the honor of having the time to say goodbye to those I love. To do the things I want to do! To color my hair the crazy red I've always wanted! To write a memoir (truly, I am!)! To tell people about Stiff Person Syndrome affecting the heart, so the next generation doesn't have to die from it! To tell Tom all I ever wanted him to know and how grateful I am for his love!

There is beauty in this!! There is honor!! There can be joy, even fun!

I had the very best life! No regrets. I had lows, but my highs were truly amazing. My highs rocked! I feel as though I've lived 100 lives. I trust heaven is going to be amazing! I know my pup Simon, my (step)Mom, Jennifer, and more people I love are going to be there.

I want to be sure I don't shy away from saying goodbyes or being uncomfortable. This is not a time to feel uncomfortable. This is part of life. It is real! I've decided that I am okay with this, I just need love and family and friends to get me through.

I am sad thinking about leaving my Tom and my babies behind. That will break my heart. I hope I've showed my nieces, nephews, and godchildren a little about love from my perspective. I miss them so much. My friends know how much I love them! *The Write Review*....no words. Do I cry about all of this? Of course! But, I am at peace! I promise!

And, please don't feel sorry for me. My life is wonderful! I'm so loved, and so many people dream of such love.

I still have so much to share with you.

If only love could save me.

My life has its purpose. I trust God has his plan!

I Want My Wings Back

I had plans.
Goals. Entertainment Lawyer.

My steps were planned.
Beautifully. Heading to Berkeley.

Too many pills to count.
Infusions every week. Sometimes more.
At 32 surgeries, I stopped counting.

Too many lost friends.
I know it's hard to
be friends with me.

Interrupting my goals.
Or is it the diseases,
Eating away at my nerve's fibers
and brains transactions never fully realized.

Dizziness. Falls.
Agony. Stiffness.
Organs not working
or communicating with my brain.

I will not let any of this take my smile away.
Too many reasons to live.

Edema is so heavy.
Uncomfortable.
Often feeling like dragging another body.

End stage?
Did you say this is the ending of me?
4th Quarter.

I accept this, and
I don't all at the same time.

I'm not giving up.

I want my wings back.
I'll always choose life.

You'd like me to try a new drug?
Even if I'm the first,
And my mission is to just bring hope
to the next warriors.

If I am swallowed
up into the heavens
just know
each step I took was
hard, and beautiful.

I never gave up.
And I never gave in.

I just went home.
Riding on a dandelion seed.
From the wish of a child.

Misfiring of My Heart

(The night before my heart surgery. Still trusting its strength yet concerned because I was abandoned by some of its biggest loves. Pondering all my recent loss of friends, while celebrating all I had. Praying the hurt won't affect how I make it through the surgery.)

My heart beats loud and hard,
A reminder of its pain and sorrow.
Feeling like the beat I should only hear at a funeral,
with tears falling, stinging my eyes
as they turned red with pain.

My heart is powerful and strong,
loving fiercely and proudly.
I trust this is what empowers me.
Beautiful Aurora lights shining outward,

Sometimes love is just not enough.
and sometimes, it is just too much.
I chose the biggest love and lost so much.

The pounding slices like warning signs.
Excessive deep breathing, that hurts,
feeling like leftover embers of flames from the lies.

Attached to those bridges left burning
always thrown at my feet
in a wake of mistakes and regrets
that have always arrested forgiveness.

Electric misfiring of my heart.

Little sparks of light.

Some people see me and care,

Others are just blind and empty.

Some have simply forgotten me,
and our cherished memories.

Five decades of proven devotion
thrown away.
Like me and my heart
are garbage.

Proving love is definitely not enough.

59

Ad for Simon's Items

(imaginary because I donated his things)

*P*ay it forward exchange for thirty to thirty-five pound dog items: If you don't have a dog yet, maybe you are ready to adopt a dog? Are you a really loving person?

I have items that came from love that are hoping to be loved again. All gently used but taken care of with love.

Beginning with a medium-size dog crate, full of toys, and a medium-size bed. There is also oatmeal dog shampoo. Simon's winter coat with the fluffy hood, his winter boots that we walked miles in (we loved the snow), his raincoat, and about a dozen sweaters, and a sign that says "Dog Avenue." Every dog home needs this adorable sign.

He has been gone five years, one month, and fifteen days, and I'm trusting that I can pass on his items now. I have cherished them, all these years without him. They are priceless.

I can't believe I'm finally ready to pass them on.

Suddenly it feels like a crime to have them just sitting here when a dog could be using them. All of his things look lonely and sad, so they must be passed on. My heart is smart enough to know that if another dog can fall in love with these things, they'll come alive again.

Maybe having them out of the house will help my heart heal a little bit quicker. This five-plus year endless heartache needs to heal.

Simon loved our walks as much as I did. He never complained about my overzealous care and love and protection of him. There wasn't a thing I wouldn't do for Simon. There wasn't a thing he wouldn't do for me.

One time he jumped in a lake, and I was right behind him. My motherly instincts took over, and I didn't even hesitate. This part of the lake didn't even reach my knees but I dove into this water, and both Simon and I ended up soaking wet. My friends couldn't believe how fast I was in that water. I loved him with an intensity that was hard to explain. We were bonded, connected, partnered as if we were truly mother and child. I still wonder if there's a difference between an infant and a dog. I believe the love feels the same, but I am not a mother of a human baby so I could be wrong.

Everyone told me he would never wear the winter boots I got him, but he did. I put them on him for the first time, and he looked at me with eyes that said, "I know you want me to wear these so I will. But I'm not happy about this."

Could you accept these items and share them with your dog with the same amount of love and attention that I did?

I always say that grief is just love turned inside out. That's why this hurts. I'll be letting this love walk out my door with you. Please promise the items will be cherished.

Because of this, I would truly love to see these items go to a loving dog Mama or Papa. Simon loved his sweaters, so they must be used with tender loving care, and I hope to God that the new dog walks around with pride wearing those sweaters. I don't know what it was, but Simon would get so excited when I pulled out the sweaters. But he was never happier than in his Notre Dame or Jets Jersey. I think he knew they were gifts from his uncle. But feel free to pass them on if your dog doesn't like them.

Every item included is in excellent condition. These were all well taken care of just as I took care of Simon. They were my baby's things because Simon was my little boy in a sense. He made me feel loved in a way that I never could understand before meeting him. A love that truly has your cup runneth over and has you saying I love you to the moon and back over and over again.

I'd like to offer the items to someone who will pay it forward. Maybe you would choose to volunteer at One Love Dog Rescue, or donate funds. I volunteer for them calling my work #OperationSimon because his love still needs to be shared. Working with the rescue gave me an outlet for his huge love. Isn't that what animal rescue is all about?

It's about love. It's about leaving no dog behind. It's about listening to the voices of dogs that can't speak, because they do talk to you. I always knew what Simon needed and what he wanted.

But the day that he had to go to heaven he looked at me in such a way that said "Mama, it's time and it's okay." And the greatest gift I could give him was to say goodbye and let him go.

So, this is a pay-it-forward exchange. We can make the exchange this Saturday at the One Love Dog Rescue adoption event at Petco. I'll send the details once an agreement is reached.

I hope you find the same love I did. You can have a dog at home already that you're madly in love with, or maybe you'll adopt a dog at this One Love Dog Rescue event on Saturday.

Love walked in, and it truly never left. When Simon was gone, we adopted three large dogs to share Simon's love with.

Are you understanding how much love Simon had? We had to adopt three dogs until we felt the same fulfillment our little Simon gave us.

I can't imagine my life without our Daphne, Bonnie, and Sullivan now.

That's the beauty of a dog's love. It moves throughout your body, and it can last a lifetime in your heart. A dog's love is so profound, it transcends time.

Only serious inquiries please. As stated earlier, all items are priceless, and we want them to go to a kind and loving home.

Our Daphne Needed Bonnie

(Daphne was adopted from Last Hope and Bonnie was adopted from One Love Dog Rescue.)

Transforming a confused rescued dog takes:

• Patience

• Proper training

• and, at times, the companionship of another dog that will teach the rescued dog (who may never have lived INSIDE a home with a family) how to relax and what is expected of a well-mannered pet.

Our Southern transport dog, Daphne Moon is from Kentucky, rescued as part of the Hurricane Harvey "clear the shelters" mission. Daphne looks like a Golden Retriever, but when we ran her DNA we discovered she was Great Pyrenees and White Swiss Shepherd. These breeds were bred to do different tasks. Pyrenees are often left outside to guard the flock in rural areas.

Bonnie Love, the smaller dog, was a One Dog Love Rescue Inc. foster from Alabama who came into our home (and stayed) after Daphne fell in love with her. Bonnie showed her big sister the ropes of proper dog decorum and helped her settle into our home.

Here is a note I sent to Last Hope. We were so grateful that they sent Sandy to us. She was an amazing trainer.

"I had to share the last few wonderful months we've had with Daphne (aka Daisy while at Last Hope). You sent your trainer Sandy to me when I was ready to surrender her, believing she deserved a better home than I could provide for her.

Thank you for offering Sandy to evaluate us. Her tools were amazingly helpful. I was surprised how much I needed the training.

The best choice I ever made was committing myself to her training and also adopting a dog named Bonnie we were fostering from One Love Dog Rescue. Sandy suggested another dog could help Daphne learn social skills with people. I think they needed each other.

Our house is the happiest place ever.

I now volunteer at a rescue and work vigilantly helping people find ways to have a better relationship with their dogs when they are scared they may have made the wrong choice.

Sandy taught me so much, so now I am passing it on. I thought you'd like to know how happy Daphne is, and how truly full my heart is with her in my life. My cup runneth over."

Last Hope posts this on Daphne's adoption day each year to inspire other people not to give up on their dog so easily. Admittedly, I was almost one of them.

Once I taught Daphne what she needed, our lives together have been perfect. I wouldn't change a thing. We have even added a third dog, named Sullivan. Our pack is perfect.

61

What Friendship Is to Me

Friendship is a lot like a marriage agreement,
Because ultimately loving someone in your life
is a choice.
You choose to love them in sickness and in health,
For richer and for poorer,
In good times and in bad.

That's the agreement I make in my heart
when I call you my friend.

I've lost so many friends along the way
It's been heartbreaking.
People I've loved the most.
People I would've done anything for,
who betrayed me, and I never saw it coming.

Now, I try to surround myself with people who choose to always
champion me,
always support me,
and surround me with their light
when mine can't shine.

People I promise to do the same for.

People who remember to always say thank you,
because I'll do the same.
People who will remember me,
even if I am falling ten feet behind,
People who choose to never let me feel "less-than."

People I promise to do the same for.

The people still hanging onto me fiercely are these people!
The ones who always think I am amazing,
even when I was simply the best I could be.

The ones who forgave me when I made mistakes.
The ones who helped hold me up as I was sliding,
especially with my diseases instead of forgetting about me
and treating me as if I let them down.

These are the friends I hold dear,
because they are the very definition of friendship.

That's what friendship is to me.

62

A Triple Dog Love

The powerful look of a rescue dog!

Every once in a while I get this look from Sullivan
and all see is love looking back at me.
He is not speaking.
He is not moving.
Simply staring.
For a long time.
Very intense.
So powerfully
All I know is that I am
so grateful I am his mama,

And I trust he knows this.
I feel like he is repeating
"I love you, I love you, I love you,"
All day long.

Every once in a while I get this look from Bonnie,
And all I see is love staring back at me.
She never barks,
she only talks.
I always know what she wants,
By the simple glint in her eyes.
And she always puts her head on my shoulder
or my arm.
I find comfort being her mama.
I trust she knows this.
I feel like she keeps repeating
"thank you, thank you, thank you"
All day long.

Every once in a while I get a look from Daphne,
And all I see is love staring back at me.

She's at my feet,
she's protecting me.
Simply guarding,
simply watching,
so powerfully.
All I know is that I am
so grateful she is my protector.
And I trust she knows this.
I feel like she is repeating,
"you're safe, Mama, you're safe"
All day long.

Silence Is Deadly

The silence is so deafening
I am reminded of that frightful sound
that you hear when you're under the water
and you are so aware of the loneliness.

No one is listening,
it's complete nothingness.

The silence that cracks houses
breaks the people down Like a house of cards
that will never be in the same box again.
It is the loudest, most painful silence.

There is a card missing from my life,
because nobody listened
to our cries for help.

She is dead.
Her card is lost
and cannot ever be played again.

I visit her grave,
and try to keep it pretty.

I will never be silenced again!
Now, I must fight for Jennifer's voice.
It has become one of my life's biggest endeavors.

My home will have no cracks,
It will not tumble down.
I will be sure anyone who comes to us for
respite, refuge, or care
will always be welcomed and heard
and witnessed.

No one will die because they were silenced.

There will be forgiveness.

My inner circle will be
part of the solution.
Our love will sustain us all.

My Warrior Spirit

Some of the people in my life choose to never see my warrior spirit or its value. It is enough that I believe. I am finally seeing my worth, my value and my life. I am *Willow Sky!*

I have been told I am lazy, a pin cushion to doctors. I've heard "I'm sick of you being sick" so often, it doesn't shock me anymore. I have been bullied by people whom I thought were kind. I've been shamed for failing to get over my traumas. Meanwhile professionals say that the type of traumas that I experienced are the kind that you do not get over. You have to learn to live with them. I live with mine by still going to counseling.

I am judged for being on disability. Someone who was supposed to love me compared me to someone else and said, "She gets unwell as much as you, but she keeps going to work and doesn't give up." I dare them to be me.

From breaking my neck and having to leave college.

Having to leave work because of disability, to keeping up with *The Write Review* blog and starting an online book club. I began interviewing authors. I had to keep myself busy even if I couldn't move around well.

I never gave up or gave in.

I am in for the fight of my life, and I'm calling upon my warrior spirit more than ever before. I'm also calling upon my friends and family who choose to support me. The ones who see my value. I need you more than you can imagine.

I ask that you trust in the knowledge that I'm smart and a true advocate for myself, so I've certainly researched every corner of the earth. I ask that you trust that I've tried everything to get rid of this pain and deal with my disease. I ask that you trust that I have assembled a great team of doctors. They are taking care of me, knowing I am an amazingly smart patient. They are all so proud of me. I know because they tell me this.

I know it probably looks crazy that I'm planning events so far ahead with this prognosis. But I'm envisioning myself still alive. I'm seeing myself doing these things. I'm planning. I must have a purpose.

Some people make me feel like they wish I was dead. Like I'm not a survivor! I feel sorry for the people who wish I was no longer here. I'm sorry that you don't see the beauty in my life. You are the one missing out. I'm so grateful I'm learning my self-worth and not letting people bring me down anymore.

I must have a goal other than death. While they say I am in the end stages of Stiff Person Syndrome, I am fighting. There is beauty in truly living while I'm here.

There is so much love in all of my friends helping me along the way. This love sustains me. I know them by their love!

65

Circle of Life Ends With Me

The prompt was to use our favorite word with a new definition.

My life (two words). N. A relationship with myself, learning my value along the way. Loving myself and others.

Extraordinary. Adj. Word from the quote "Choose to Be Extraordinary" that was ingrained into my head at High Point University. This became a goal in life. Especially after learning I would not become a mom.

Mom. N. Everything I've missed in this life and wished someone called me.

Extravaganza. N. The extra "sauce" I always made sure was in my life. I guess that sauce was called "Vaganza."

Guadalajara. N. A classmate of mine wrote a story about going to medical school in Guadalajara and ever since then I say Guadalajara anytime I want to smile.

Spoiler. N. Getting advance notice that I am in the end stage of my disease. Knowing I have to prepare for my death because it is eminent. I plan everything and share it with all the people I love because now I need I have become the very thing I always hated in book reviews: a spoiler.

Loss. N. Everything I am thinking about and feeling right now as I sit in the hospital again.

Mahalo. N. The Hawaiian word for thank you that I adore. It is the word that will be on my celebration of life cards.

In a moment of sadness, I think:

I imagine
my life could have been extraordinary

if I had become a mom.
It would've been an extravaganza every day.
I would've taken my children to Guadalajara.
Praying along the way there would be no spoiler alerts needed
and we would never suffer any loss too soon.

But I'm not going to live that way!

So actually,
my life has been extraordinary.
I have mothered many children,
and I live an extravaganza,
making the hospital my Guadalajara.
And I'll always announce spoiler alerts about my health,
because any loss of me shouldn't hurt knowing I will be out of pain, and
I've left in a Vaganza!

The Circle of life ends with me.

I Could Have Used a Win Today

While I wasn't in favor of the possibility of needing open heart surgery going into yesterday's procedure, I was hoping all I might need was a stent and/or fluid removal from my lungs or heart, so that today would be a new day for me. Instead, I lay here, the same, with a sore area where I now have stitches. My heart isn't sore physically from where they explored, but I do feel an open wound of pain that is hurting so deeply, they may has well have cut my heart in two. My heart is broken. Cracked wide open. I could've used a win.

You see, I've been sick with autoimmune diseases since I was 18-years-old, and quite frankly, I'm tired. I thought for once I was going to have the easy fix. My new normal has reached its highest peak and I need to learn acceptance again. I need to also pray it doesn't escalate. I've lost muscle tone in my eyelids and the left side of my face. I can't walk far or do anything without being unable to breathe, shaking, having my neck, jaw, and tongue go stiff. I'll foam at the mouth or vomit if I push it. It's awful.

My doctor determined my enlarged heart isn't being caused by a clogged artery or fluid or infection, and the inflamed lungs were not caused by fluid or infection. The aortas that they were concerned about being inverted aren't, thank God! Only regurgitating minimally.

If it was a mechanical fix, that would be easy. This autoimmune stuff, no. The surgeon even apologized to me while I was on the table as tears rolled down my face, and he told the nurse, Kip, to give me more calming medications in my IV. I was becoming emotional knowing nothing could help. These diseases were winning.

I've had worse days though. I had to have a total hysterectomy when I was 23 because endometriosis just took everything, making me feel like I was no longer a woman. That was by far the worst. No one believed me for so long when I was sick that they let it get that bad. I was the one who paid a surgeon to look to see if I had it. I've always been my only advocate. Not even my closest loved ones were there to support me.

No one stood by my side. I was always made to be uncomfortable.

Immunodeficiency is the complete opposite of autoimmunity! My body is in a state of confusion all the time. So many people do not know the difference.

When I went to a Mayo Clinic, (by the grace of donations of friends and family for the stay) who had me visit for three weeks under a special program for people with multiple illnesses, I finally got some answers. I learned that I was born with the immunodeficiency. When I broke my neck in a car accident at age 18, spinal fluid leaked into my bloodstream and caused an infection. This infection never received treatment, which then caused the autoimmune diseases to begin....one-by-one, feeding the next. I have an amazing team of doctors here who work as a team, and we can connect with my team at Mayo at any time. I came home from Mayo with a treatment plan....and here we are today.

People still offer their celery juice or low this or low that diets and essential oil promises. Trust me, I have tried them all! I even became an integrative nutritionist so I could learn to eat healthier for myself. I started taking herbs good for Hashimoto's disease for example, and I landed myself in the hospital for eight days because I had an adverse reaction to it. I'm 50. Trust me, I'm rocking these diseases like a champion! Don't think for one moment I'm not a warrior. My doctors say everything I live with is difficult, but I typically manage with a smile on my face.

We knew all along things could keep progressing regardless of the treatments. Nevertheless, we had hoped for longer timeframes between full organ involvement. My heart and lungs were still in the clear. Until July 10th. They were shocked at the changes. Again, suddenly the heart was enlarged, lungs inflamed, showing ischemia and ischemic dilation during the stress test, and my doctor saw my neck and jaw go stiff, and being unable to speak.

They determined this had to be a mechanical issue. If my record showed anything I should have known that no stent or blood thinners would ease this for me. We already knew my treatments were super aggressive with the IVIG and 1500 mg in steroids last week, the treatments made no changes.

I really could've used a win at the cardiac catheterization today. I cry because they couldn't fix my heart. I'm losing this battle. I'm not ready to surrender yet. I have too many things I want to do in this life. I want to keep loving my husband, pups, and cats. I want to watch my nieces and nephews grow up.

I could've used a win today.

67

I Am Always Looking for Love

*L*ove.

I am always looking for love. There should be bins of it sold at secondhand shops for people in need of love, maybe un-mothers, un-fathers, and un-daughters could find one another and there would be a lot less loneliness in this world. I wish we had the ability to swipe left and right to fulfill that need for love like lovers do on Tinder. It is just as powerful. It is just as needed. I could use a parent who would want to visit when the doctor says you can die at any time.

I was never favored. I was only wanted when needed. I was more of a helper. Love.

You can't be loved right when you were unplanned. I could feel it. The unloving. It was so palpable, it hurt. It made the home murky and thick. Never comfortable. Reminding me of the mistake I was.

We moved almost every year, Ireland being my favorite when I was five.

Leaving my closest best friend from second grade. My blood sister. We did everything together. Leaving her meant a huge loss of love. I couldn't say goodbye.

Love.

I wish I could buy it like a vowel on *Wheel of Fortune*. I wish I could've just bought some when I watched this game show with my grandmother every Wednesday.

Love never worked around me when I was younger, and I believed it was all because of me.

Love.

I want to be wrapped in a blanket that I never have to remove. I wanted it to feel like a hug.

I wish I could go to a store and just buy some hugs.

I wanted something to soothe me because nothing ever does. I've bought rattles from my shaman tribe. My counselor says it was because I probably soothed myself as a baby with rattles.

Love.

"I'd like a gallon of love today or could I get a quart of that or could you refill this pint until it empties, and I'll be back for a refill." But you can't do that with love; you either have it or you don't.

I was always chasing it. Like a marathon runner or just trying to pass the baton.

I tried to love myself. I'm still trying. I'm too sensitive; this is why I struggle.

Hard to do when you survived your best friend's murder. Survivor's guilt eats away at self-love. I could've died four days before, but here I am. Feeling unloved. Unworthy. Guilty for being alive.

Love.

Depression. You're sold right next to love. To me, they are so close.

Depression surrounded me until I met my (step)Mom. She loved me like she would be so proud to be my real life parent. She loved me so much; I knew love with her.

She was everything. She was my "I walked into a store and bought her as a gift for myself."

If only this love didn't have to die with her. I feel it often, but it is no longer a call away. I need her like I need air. She knew my love reserve would be empty and I would be searching for love when she died. My (step)Mom wrote to my friend and asked that they keep loving me, because I need love like I need air. She knew me, because she cared to know me.

Love.

I learned from my (step)Mom so much about love.

It can't be bought because it's free. Just look around. I bet someone is offering you honest true love. You are just not seeing it.

Look harder.

Open the door to the shop and enter. Swipe right. Do something. Love is there.

Even if it is only in the mirror looking back at you.

You must start there.

Love.

Love yourself first.

You have value. "Annie, you are mine!"

I loved her so much.

Love.

A word search I can't find.

But I'm not giving up.

I know love is with me.

68

Thoughts After Holding a Rock

I have a rock.
Aware of my burdens.
Aware of the letters I need and must write before my last breath.
Aware of my love.
Each stone within it is one of the lives I lead until now.
Some are big, some are small.
Some are shiny, some are matte.
All earth charms reminded me of the shamanism
I practice that brings me closer to Spirit, Mother Earth, and God.
Reminding me to reach into that tool box
I made for for my spirit guide and spirit animal totems,
and all the tools to help ground me.
Always adding to it; is a wondrous thing.
I feel the heaviness of this one rock,
a reflection of my body.
It is full of water that is not flowing properly
with several doctors trying to figure it out before it's too late.

It is also the weight of loss I'll leave behind
to those who love me, especially my dogs
Daphne, Bonnie, and Sullivan.

Please don't betray me.
This rock is becoming so important to me
as I beg for healing.
Yet, it reminded me of the surface of the moon
where I imagine my heaven to be.
Where my loved ones who have passed are waiting on me.

I imagine living my life.
To see my ZTA big sisters Jill and Julie again,
For they both bring so much love to my life,
just as all my ZTA sisters do.

In my toolbox there is kindness and smiles,
Charissa can be found here.
I met her at a bonfire party and we all
went swimming! One of my favorite memories.
Sonya is seen here, too. She is nothing
but a smiling, joyfully kind person.
I am so blessed to know Charissa and Sonya
and call them friends.

There are also friends like Kimberlee and
Ann-Marie with their gorgeous children.
John and Virginia and their hysterical kids,
Hannah and JJ, being my godson.
Same goes for Karen and Matt and their kids,
Joey and my goddaughter, Ayla! Also,
my godson Trevor! I adore his family.
I adore him and his mom, Janelle, and brother, Aiden.
I love all of these families and miss them the same.
I often wish I could visit with them.
I whisper this into the rocks.
I may not get to visit, but hopefully they know my love.

Macy my penpal! Oh! I'm just so behind, my love.
I love watching you grow and hearing from you.

I hope you can all forgive me.

This rock can carry my burdens and shortcomings,
And offer me forgiveness.

I hope my friends can feel it,
So, all they can feel is the love I'm sending.

I trust in the life energy of
This rock and that rock!

Welcome Back, WILLOW SKY

For years I only saw myself
as a bunch of rocks
piled into a wired frame of a body
hunched over in agony,
one on top of the other
haphazardly.

Not able to escape
because I can barely move.
Everything hurts.
All parts feel broken.
I am stuck.

But I can decide
that these rocks are glorious stones.

They are beautiful, not ugly
or necessarily confining.

I can see a more stunning
and balanced statue.
One I can move slowly with grace.
One I can remind myself is still
Here and functioning.

One still fighting!

I am a shaman*, after all.

I admire and revere stones.
They each have a soul
and heartbeat of their own.
I see them free, with
no cages around them.

With room to grow and
blessed through my
faith.
Surviving through all the
Love I receive.

There is hope.
I see it.
I feel it.
I believe it.

No matter how mobile
I am,
I am a lot more beautiful
than that hunched over pile of rocks.

I am a woman full of stone,
proudly being my true self.

My *tribe named me **Willow**
for I am strong like
the willow tree withstanding
every storm,

and *Sky*, because I truly see,
accept and love
everyone with a
heart as big as the sky.

I almost forgot about her.

Thank you, Tribe,
For reminding me
of my truest strength..
Welcome back, *Willow Sky!*

*Peruvian Q'ero Tribe (Medicine Wheel)

70

My Accidental Friendship

*"All endings are also beginnings.
We just don't know it at the time."*

— Mitch Albom

S uns do set. Lights do go out. I felt a little lost.

"How lucky I am to have something that makes saying goodbye so hard." We had to say goodbye to Serena as part of *"The Write Review."*

Serena and I met when we were set up as book buddies with Brenda Novak's Book Club. It was a simple pairing that accidentally became a lifetime friendship. I knew right away that I liked Serena. She was so kind.

Serena and I decided we would try to grow our own book club to share our love of books and authors with others. We began with ten ladies and had our first live chat with an author we both love, Bette Lee Crosby. Now there are more than 2,000 members.

She is absolutely one of my best friends. I am blessed because I trust that will not change. I love Serena dearly. She is very good to me.

She did so much work for *The Write Review*, its members and authors, from spreadsheets to helping me with live events! To her posts! To her reviews! So much more! She held everything together. She was the glue.

The Write Review has always had so much heart. We were built on a foundation of kindness and friendship. We've always been about book reviews! Our genres included thriller, historical fiction, literary fiction and women's fiction, with some paranormal, fantasy and a few downright scary books in there, too.

I've enjoyed the pleasure of sharing other groups that I like here. I've recommended other book groups and clubs, reviewers, and interviewers to authors all the time. I have tried to teach people as much as I can when they asked.

We will always try to be up and running. Thank you, Serena, for all you have done to build this community.

You are truly special.

You are truly admired.

You are truly loved.

You will forever be woven into the fabric of *The Write Review* because you are woven into the fabric of my life.

"If you're brave enough to say goodbye, life will reward you with a new hello." – Paulo Coelho

We are friends for a lifetime. She is always with me, even though we live far apart.

We say good morning every day, which is so special. We are two peas in a pod. But, she doesn't drink coffee. I'll never understand that. Haha!

Prayers and Tissues

"**A**nnie! Stop making such a big deal about this. I know you're not going to die anytime soon. Come on, I could die just crossing the street sometime today!"

So many people say some version of this to me one way or another. It really hurts. It makes me feel like I shouldn't mention what I'm going through or my emotions. I have so many. I'm stressed. I'm scared. I feel so alone.

Did I do all I want to do? Are you thinking of these things?

I try to gently and kindly respond with "Please don't Doctor Google my diseases, because what you don't understand is I have many. Even my doctors don't understand them. Put them all together in one body, and they aren't the same as dealing with one. Can't you see this?"

I am actually planning my end-of-life care, and my after end-of-life care. It's overwhelming when people repeatedly deflect my pain and respond with some variation of: "Well, we should all be making these plans."

I think to myself: *Well, I don't believe that you're making your 'I just died crossing the street' plans, are you? Do you live daily feeling like you are on the edge of death?*

I've learned by the high percentage of responses from my family and friends that I am just to go on as if I will absolutely be here tomorrow. Empathy cannot be taught to most of the people I love. You should see how much they care about others that get as sick. That hurts more than knowing death is a breath away.

Visit me? Make me feel a little more loved? Actually call me? I am expecting too much.

Not many people know what it takes for me to just get through the day. I think one of the hardest things that I hear is: "But, you look or sound so good." My reaction to this comment is *How does one look at the last stage of their life?*"

I have to prove I'm sick enough to be loved through this. You'd be surprised how many would rather I be dead already. They don't understand that I don't have an ETA on rising to Heaven. They aren't proud of how hard I am fighting. Didn't they learn anything from when I had endometriosis and was called a hypochondriac for years and put on lithium?

Until my last breath I will be wishing I was understood.

All I want is love, compassion, and to still be able to laugh and enjoy life.

I'm trapped in a house, trapped in a room, trapped on the couch, trapped in a body. I'm losing my memory. Each organ is miscommunicating with the other, most especially my brain. I can feel each synapse going off incorrectly, especially between my brain and heart. The dizziness feels like a black hole.

It's like feeling my heartbeat is not talking correctly to my soul. Mismatching with a pounding sensation. My body's music is off. I close my eyes, and it is screaming for help. It's in a constant argument. It doesn't turn off because the reset is not working. I don't ever feel peace. I am trying desperately to reach for it. My body's soul has so much more to do.

A loved body fights hard and strongly with a fire I can feel. I need help keeping it lit, not extinguished. Not thrown away like garbage. Not ignored. Still celebrated, honored, and loved. There are friends who help my strength.

The people who don't walk this path gently and with grace with me chip away at my energy field. The people who love me along the way are the ones who will keep me here longer. I am so grateful for love like it is my food and I'm starving,

I have learned to align my chakras and more from Denise, a dear ZTA sorority sister. I have glorious distance Reiki sessions from another of my sorority sisters Cathlyn. I try to envision my brain telling my heart what to do in the right way and so on. I've been taught how to spin my energy fields to open them up and get them moving properly. I do that each and every day and so much more from what Denise has taught me. Denise is my soul advisor. From mantras to music, she reaches my soul. There is so much power in keeping that healthy. There is so much fire in their desire to see me live on.

I've gone off my meds and been put back on them at Mayo Clinic. I often hear, "You take too much medication" from people who don't know me enough to say that.

I've even been told that essential oils can heal my immunodeficiency. All these people seriously miss the fact that I don't make my own antibodies. I need human antibody donations infused into my bloodstream. Why am I continually explaining myself?

I do listen because I do get a lot of wonderful advice. I use essential oils properly every day for reasons besides my immunodeficiency, thanks to one of my closest friends, Serena. She keeps me fully stocked. I use sacred Hindu Vibhuti Ash. Practice with Tibetan music bowls, I pray to Jesus, to God, Mother Mary and Angels. I pray to Mother Earth and various powers within the universe. I pray harder and longer during a full moon with ceremonies involving crystals and feathers and stones in more ways than you can even imagine. I burn sage and palo santo. I practice angel and other energy healings, Intuit oracle and tarot cards. I have an altar at home.

I became a certified integrative nutritionist. I became a Shaman with the Q'ero Peruvian Tribe. My given name is Willow Sky, because I am as strong as the willow tree that survives many storms, and I love all I can see in this world.

I trust someone or something out there above or beside me is listening and hearing me. I'm not going to give up. I'm a Warrior with a huge army alongside me. I have faith and hope.

There is one thing I universally request because I believe they are heard: I always request prayers and tissues. For myself and my loved ones. We can all use prayers! I can certainly always use tissues!

Imagine a world where we all prayed and cared for one another at all times.

Prayers and tissues always accepted. Loving advice accepted. Stop with the side glances, or the sarcasm in your voice. If you question me, please just walk away from my life. You don't deserve to know me. You don't deserve my love.

Love heals. That is what I'm looking for. I want to live and love for a long time.

 72

Sour Grapes

My name goes down their
throats like sour grapes.
They never see goodness in me.

He has completely wiped me out.
I could walk the plank for them
and that ugly person would still say
I take my loved ones for granted.

Plenty know that's not true.

I wanted to rent a plane
carrying a sign behind it saying
"I'm available to be loved,
I want to belong"

Knowing so many secrets,
I'm to lock away with a lost key.
They feel none of our story should be shared.

I always come out looking bad anyway.
It's these secrets that will kill me.

But I'll turn their sour grapes,
into wine just for me and my loving friends
who trust I don't take them for granted

and we will savor the taste together.

The Bottomless Bag of Love From My ZTA Sisters

I was admitted to the hospital because I now have to add congestive heart
failure to my itinerary of illnesses to battle. I am starting to get depressed
now because I can feel my life slipping away. There were a lot of hospital stays
and more parts of me breaking down, like I was a used car getting ready for
the junk yard. I have become popular at the hospital and that is not good, but
it does help when I needed something.

My sorority sisters left me a bag full of things I could use to walk this path
with a brighter feeling. They'll always be with me. I reached in and pulled
out LOVE.

I wished on so many dandelions in high school, hoping to become a Zeta. I knew when I went to visit High Point College for my presidential scholarship interview that I wanted to be a Zeta. They were so wonderful to me when I visited. I met Jill, who became my Big Sister. They took me to a party at the fraternity house, on the Theta Chi floor.

There would be no other sorority for me, and I knew that. I suicided ZTA, which means they were the only sorority I chose on Bid Day, the final day of a recruitment period when bids are distributed. Bid Matching is a system for matching the choice of a potential new member with the choice of a chapter. I was invited to join more than ZTA, so only checking off ZTA meant that, that's it. You are not in a sorority. If you chose a second and third choice that invited you, you had the opportunity to be part of another. The stars were aligned. I knew these girls were special. All these years later, I know it is true.

Grief is just love turned inside out. It is painful. I am carrying the grief of losing the old me and now being unable to get around well. For it is always there. It never says goodbye. It is thick and hot, almost molten, because it burns from my heart like a flame. Embers of memories flying everywhere. My sisters want me to look at it as time. To remember to make the most of each day.

Next, I pull out GRIEF. My grief is everywhere. Just like my love.

Grief feels like all the cells in the universe that are pulsating in the air helping me breathe are somehow short-circuiting. I am left breathless. It's love that serves as my oxygen. It helps me sustain myself. It's my ZTA sisters helping to hold me up.

Their love is like standing under a huge waterfall that's just all encompassing, surrounding me with liquid love pouring over me. I can't walk away from it. It feels so lavish and opulent. I can physically feel grief turning inside and outside and upside-down becoming love. My grief is no longer hurting when I'm there. Because its tears pouring over me can't be compared to raindrops anymore. This is huge and powerful and mighty. The pain is washing away. (I pretend I'm doing this in the shower, when I feel I can't find their love. It is there, I just need to look deeper.) They want me to wash away the grief I'm carrying with this bar of lavender soap they gave me. They offer the chance to get rid of GRIEF, so I can see that I can live without it.

Tom opens the door to leave for work, and he says, "Annie, Your ZTA sisters were here!" I get up and see that they have put ZTA ♥ ZLAM across our front lawn. I cry. I always said ZLAM, (Zeta Love and Mine) in college. I know Dana-Lynn is doing all of this work. My ZTA sisters are totally SPOILING me. There is no limit to this. Dana-Lyn is an angel delivering things to me.

The smell of wisteria reminds me of what feels like a thousand memories, only I'm in a field of them. I am not just standing in front of a wisteria bush on my friend's patio at a party. They make me tear up as my mind flips through movies of us in summertime. It feels like warm, soft hugs are coming to me one by one. Each person saying hello. My grieving is love. It is love walking around on earth sending messages to heaven. I can't ever lose the love of our memories. My friends will carry it via their favorite scents. They gave me wisteria, lavender, and sandalwood. My friend Vinny Spinnato has a Certified Nose. I wonder if these scents would mix well.

They gave me HOPE. Their constant letters and cards, saying, "you got this!" made me believe them. My ZTA Big Sister, Jill, sent me tons of cards, as did Laura, Noelle, and others. It was so much fun to get mail.

Then I was given COMFORT. It was soft blankets. These blankets wrap me in their love and keep them close. I could bring one to my infusion. The girls would flicker in my mind like an old black and white movie. I could hear the rhythm of the film running through the projector. I always loved that feeling. I won't ever lose this comfort.

I am reminded of the time we all went to the Dollar Theatre to see *Dirty Dancing*. We loved that movie.

I reach in one more time and pull out a slinky…I named it HUMOR. There was lastly a PRAYER Box! I take it with me everywhere, so I don't miss a prayer. They love this at the hospital.

I absolutely love to laugh! When I get those deep belly laughs that make my stomach hurt and my jaw becomes almost immobile from smiling, I know that they are with me. I can feel that I am no longer laughing alone. They are always here with me in my laughter. They are still always here with me at both my good and bad times. The slinky was a toy that always made me laugh as a child. They remember.

I live in the heartbeats of my friends, especially when I need respite. Denise is my Soul Guru, Cathlyn is my Reiki Master.

I can't ever lose my ZTA sisters. They are my family, my support system.

We all must care for one another. We are really great at this. I'm no longer feeling lonely. Having reasons to live help more than anyone knows.

There will be no giving up here, for my ZTA sisters say so! My ZTA sisters, Noelle and Erica were the first people to come visit me when I was first so unwell. Erica is my biggest supporter, especially when I deal with anything medical. She has taken on this huge responsibility, and I appreciate her for this more than she knows. Noelle took me to the beach, which is on my wish list. It was great to sit in the sand and feel the salty breeze.

My ZTA sisters have given me bottomless bags and gift boxes of awesome gifts, but best of all, it was that they CARED, and they were always going to be beside me on my journey.

They are making dreams come true. A special thank you to D-L for all you do being the ELF!

Becoming a ZTA sister is one of the best things I have ever done. I am such a PROUD sister. I love my adopted Big Sister, Jules, to the moon and back. Twice. I love my Little Sister, Katie. I wish I was in contact with them more.

My sisters have given me everything that I could possibly need to work hard to keep my illnesses at bay. They have given me a FAMILY. One that always loves me.

My gratitude is immense.

ZLAM,

Annie Horsky-McDonnell

'91

I Crossed the World to Find You

(Written in dedication to my friend Connor Garrett marrying Kristel, the love of his life)

I crossed the world to find you,
but you never felt that far away.
From the moment we met I knew we were one.

I crossed the world to find you,
Your hands touched mine as if just sitting across a table.
From the moment we met, our true life began.

I crossed the world to find you,
And on the day I marry you
I choose to marry your children, too.

I crossed the world to find you.
Who knew how far our love could travel.
May our love always travel any distance.

I crossed the world to find you.
The day I marry you,
we become more than one,
for our love is immense.

I crossed the world to find you.
As you walk towards me on our wedding day,
Look into my eyes and trust nothing more than this:

I promise you arms to wrap you in love,
lips to always speak of your beauty,
and hands to always hold you in safety.

I crossed the world to find you.
You are my poetry's muse,
my life's greatest achievement.

I knew you before I met you.
I just hadn't crossed the world yet.
And I'd do it again and again and again.
For you are my world.

Today you become my wife.
My life, my love,
my promised best friend.

I crossed the world to find you,
Today we marry, and the world is at our feet.

75

Rubatosis ~ The Unsettling Awareness of My Own Heartbeat

Rubatosis! I needed to know you two weeks ago when I wrote a letter to the parole board to try to convince them to keep the man who murdered my best friend 38 years ago in prison. I've been doing this every two years for the past fourteen years. This word really could've helped me explain my deeply wounded grief. It is certainly an unsettling awareness of my very own heartbeat.

I have always said that Jennifer walks around in my heart, or she is my extra heartbeats when it's beating too fast.

Rubatosis is the perfect word because I get so unsettled. Am I not at peace because you are mad at me for living, or you want me in heaven now, or is it because you believe we both should have died at the same time? Or am I putting this on myself? This unsettling awareness of my constant 140 bpm is quite disturbing especially after surgery to slow it down. It is so confusing for even the doctors. The surgery did not work.

The moment I was told you were dead, I knew you were murdered by Robert Turley. Every cell in my body changed. Rubatosis running wild!

Each cell moved around so quickly, it felt like a cataclysmic event. I felt like I couldn't breathe, I couldn't move forward, I couldn't move backward, look up or look down, let alone speak. I realized I was just trying to get my heart to slow down. I needed it to be a normal rhythm again.

I wonder, did your soul just jump inside of mine? Did I imagine this because I couldn't let you go?

I know I was only fifteen at the time, definitely too young to comprehend my grief. At age 52, I'm still carrying the weight of losing you around with me. You aren't leaving. I am not letting you go this time.

Rubatosis became my grief's temperature gauge. My heart was beating too slowly, and I felt like I had to look for you. Then, when it was beating too fast, I felt like I was returning to you. I'll be with you soon in heaven.

I am convinced rubatosis causes early death because my grief cannot find solace anywhere. I can look as far and wide as my heart allows, but solace won't come.

Until the day I die, I will suffer from this disorganized heart, with rubatosis as my guide interfering with my brain talking to my heart.

It feels like a puzzle at a yard sale that you buy and bring home when you realize that it is missing a piece. And it will never be whole again. This is a throwaway puzzle.

Is this my throwaway life?

I try to offer myself grace. The knowledge that I will be with Jennifer again comforts me.

I thank God every day that I believe in heaven.

Rubatosis, you may win, but I will throw you away as I enter heaven.

Whispers, Wings, and Words

Whispers, Wings, and Words – *(A story dedicated to Navajo Nation's retiring Librarian, Irving Nelson written in the style of the Navajo storyteller. had a book drive in his honor.)*

Mother Earth was so full of breathtaking beauty, and she often spoke the name Irving as the leaves fell to the ground or the branches were rustling around.

One day while walking outside in a wooded area, the name Irving in a soft whisper was heard by a woman named Chenoa, her name meaning "White Dove" in the Navajo tradition. Her heart began to beat faster and faster, happily, of course. For you see, when the name is carried on the wind to be whispered in your ear, you shall soon give birth to that child.

Chenoa knew the Holy People blessed her with Irving. This would be the exact moment Chenoa would become a *shema*, meaning "mother" in the Navajo tradition.

The planning for his birth began. The members of the tribe brought generous gifts to Chenoa and her husband for their son, especially a lot of children's books. This was so that she could read to her son, even while he was in her belly, because the Navajo believe you cannot begin storytelling too soon in life.

Storytelling is one of life's greatest blessings! It shares memories, traditions, and virtues.

Chenoa was off reading to her son Irving at every moment that she could sneak away, to share even just a few words with him. She believed she could feel that he was anxious to know more about the story, so she kept trying to tell him as much as she could, and as quick as possible. He was just like her.

Maybe the true anxiety was hers because she was missing her husband, Irving's father. He had only left a few days ago, but it felt like the time spent was between here and the moon, not only a few days.

Chenoa opened her eyes one morning a few months later knowing she was going to meet her little boy Irving that day because she would be giving birth to him. Saddened when remembering her husband was not with her, she didn' t know what to do. This was such a happy time, so she needed to concentrate on Irving. This was a time of life's greatest blessings. Concentrate on this exact moment. This will be a story one day.

They had prepared a really nice room for him with a bookshelf full of books. Irving's mom was already feeling Irving's pull towards the magic of the books; she felt it was the words he was after. He would be a writer one day. She was sure of it!

That very day he was born. Chenoa immediately took his umbilical cord outside to bury it, so that he could always find his way home should he ever get lost.

When she came back, she picked Irving up to share his birth story with him. She explained to him how she was chosen to be his mother when she was walking in the woods. Next, she told him the heartbreaking story about his father's death. You see, he was a Codebreaker in World War II. He died an American hero and even though he was no longer here, it sure felt like he was.

His father's name was Onocana. It means "White Owl" in the Navajo tradition. His entire tribe believed he has taken flight into his next life but he is still watching over his family.

Onocana did write a note to Irving before he left, it said:
Son/Daughter,

Reading is a way to transport yourself to another world, another time, another dimension. Always have a book with you, always share stories and go to the library every week.

Your shizhéé, Today, tomorrow, I am with you always. Just look up.

Irving cherished this note from his shizhéé. He did as his father or shizhéé suggested! He read, shared stories, and went to the library constantly. When Irving turned eighteen, he was able to drive the bookmobile to over one hundred ten chapters! Nothing would stop him! Even a snow-storm that caused him to walk for hours in the freezing cold could not deter him.

Looking back now, forty-three years later, Irving cherishes every book he has ever handed out or recommended and all of the job titles he had until he became the top librarian.

Right now at retirement Irving realizes he just wants to know that the library will be totally fine without him. It is difficult to walk away after your life's work has been done and your time there is over.

Then one night after several moons had passed, Irving's mother left this earth and she left a very simple note for Irving, it said:

Love son, read, tell a lot of stories and always stay as kind as you are. I'll always love you from all four corners.

That night, as he sat outside looking up at the stars, the phone rang. It was David from Reader to Reader in Massachusetts, a charity organization that delivers books where they're needed. David called to tell him that there was a book community on Facebook named World of *the Write Review* that was going to hold a book drive for the Navajo Nation Library in honor of his utter dedication over the last 43 years and, of course, his retirement.

The founder, Annie, wanted him to know that as each book donation arrives they are to serve as reminders of your shema/mom, named, Chenoa, meaning "White Dove" and your shizéé/father, named, Onocona meaning "White Owl," for they'll fly into the library as if they have wings whispering into Irving's ears: "We are proud, Son and so impressed! Please stay happy! We are always loving you."

I looked up the meaning of "Irving", and it means "green river." May your life always flow as beautifully as a river, after just a little bit of rain.

Irving, you have brought so much light to the library, it is as if the sun was always shining inside the building.

May your retirement be full of travels just as gorgeous as the ones between the covers of the books you read.

We all hope you and your partner know that the books will keep being donated just as sure as the sun keeps rising.

Our Zen Dog, Bonnie Love

I'll admit, I was in love with Bonnie from the moment I saw her first photo. Then, I met her brother Clyde's foster momma, and it was like we were meant to be.

The moment I held Bonnie, I knew my heart filled again. I was to be her foster, so I knew I was in trouble!

I gave her the middle name "LOVE" even though we were only her fosters at the time. She is our zen dog. She is so calm, she rarely barks, only talks to us.

If you walked into the house with a gun to rob us and pointed it at us, she'd be like "Oh, hi! What's up? Come on in, take a seat, would you like a drink?" It's truly endearing.

We lost our dog named Simon, and my heart was completely shattered. We quickly adopted Daphne, a Pyrenees mix, a Hurricane Harvey rescue from a local shelter, Last Hope. She was struggling with PTSD and most likely never lived inside. We were working closely with a trainer because we didn't want to return her to the shelter. It was a lot of work, but we did it. She is amazing.

The trainer suggested that we foster or adopt a dog so that Daphne would have a pack of her own to care for. Bonnie helped care for the needs of Daphne's heart, while we got her ready for adoption through One Love Dog Rescue. I did not expect to adopt any of our fosters, but here we were... signing paperwork to adopt Bonnie.

Right away Bonnie and Daphne completed one another. Bonnie was exactly what Daphne needed. It was the cutest thing. If Bonnie got into trouble and was in her crate, Daphne would sit right outside the crate in front of her and vice versa. Bonnie often sat on top of Daphne to eat her treats.

It was the two of them together that filled my heart up again. I started to heal from the loss of Simon. Watching their love for one another and feeling the love they gave to me was so immensely healing and powerful. They played together, they washed each other, they snuggled, and they trained together twice a day.

Watching love inspires love! I thought I'd live with a broken heart forever. But Bonnie Love and Daphne Moon were healing it!

The most adorable part of all was that little 13-week-old Bonnie was not even at the house 12 hours and she was trying to act like a big dog like our already 3-year-old Daphne and "SIT." I have a really cute video I took the day they met. She was all about impressing Daphne and me. You can see her head held high! She was a very proud dog, and she still is.

Nothing warms the heart of a doggy momma more than seeing her babies loving one another. I knew Bonnie Love was here to stay. My heart was not walking out that front door! Thank you, One Love Dog Rescue!

We have a third loving dog from One Love named Sullivan.

The doggies love when I sing. I've written a song for them called "The Opposite of Blue." I love this song because it's perfect for everything they are.

Bonnie is also my physical aide dog. She helps me get up from the couch and often shows up like Lassie at times. If I cry, she lays her head on me. She will run from one end of the house to the other just to help me. She is like a fire truck. If she falls she falls, like Bambi, with her legs splayed out to the sides. It scares me, but it's cute at the same time.

It is because of Bonnie's love my heart has healed from the loss of Simon and it is because of her love for Daphne that her PTSD is better. It is because of her love that Sullivan thinks she is his momma pup!

Bonnie Love is love.

He Completes Us

I read to Sullivan.
I sing to Sullivan.
I always tell him the story
about how we adopted him.

We were in love with his first photo
when he was standing on his sibling,
looking at the person taking the photo.
It was evident all he wanted to do was be held.

He is a super affectionate dog,
who believes he is human.
He comes to me when it's time to go to bed,
and we snuggle all night long.

He stares at me while I sing to him.
He stares at me while I read to him.
He snuggles me when I start telling him
The story about his adoption.

I'm always honest. Tom wanted him
when he was our foster.
I wasn't sure about how I felt.
Tom said, "He is the dog for you and
he's going to snuggle you for life."

I picked him up in Queens
with all of his siblings and a few other dogs,
Transported up here from Alabama.
He is the best thing that ever happened to me.

He has me lay down if my blood pressure is high.
He does the same thing when he thinks
I've done too much.

I'm so in love with Sullivan.
I swear he is the reincarnation
of my boy, Simon.
I see it in his eyes.

I am so glad he stayed with us.
Thanking Tom for seeing what I didn't.
He completes us.

There Is a Silent Hero Among Us

*T*here's a hero I met recently; her name is Mickey Goodman. I met her because she was the ghostwriter for Vince Spinnato's memoir, *My Pursuit of Beauty*. Between the two of them, during the interview, I didn't know who I liked more. I was deeply in love with Vince's book, and I knew that they made it as a team. And when they were speaking of the book, it was obvious that they respected one another deeply, and grew to care for each other as the book came to fruition. I love when people treat each other as kindly as this. And to work on such a personal piece as a memoir together was enticing.

I knew once the interview was over that I had made two new friends, so I learned as much as I could about Vince, between his interviews, his documentary, and products made with his with his cosmetic firm.

And Mickey, I had to learn more about her as well. I quickly read another book she was the ghostwriter for called *Nine Lives of a Marriage: A Curious Journey*. This was the story of Eva Friedlander, a Holocaust survivor with one of the most original stories I've heard. It was a fabulous book. At that moment I realized that Mickey was about the story and not herself. She is so humble, gracious, kind, and talented. Besides a ton of wonderful adjectives I can use to describe her, I'm in love with her laugh!

I wanted to celebrate her with a huge event to honor her, and the amazing life she leads, especially as a journalist/writer. She told me no, I was not allowed to do it. I realized though, at that moment that I made a huge mistake: I never should've asked.

Mickey started her career in journalism when she was 59. In 2006 she broke her story in *Atlanta Magazine*. Atlanta was the number one city in the nation for child sex trafficking. She won several awards for her reporting. Over the next decade, she continued to cover this national tragedy despite receiving death threats. Her work has been published in several magazines and newspapers. She writes a regular column for a local magazine on non-profits. She is so talented; she has served on the Board of the American Society of journalism and Authors (ASJA). She rebooted the Atlanta Chapter of ASJA and is the chapter president. I'd like to add that when she makes suggested edits, you make them. I know I sure did.

Mickey is my hero because she is a genuinely kind person. She thinks of other people whether it was breaking a story on a child sex trafficking ring or writing stories as a ghostwriter for people who are not ready to write their own story. She helps them get the words out.

It's often the quiet people who do things humbly and with love who are doing things that will often surprise you. Mickey is that person. The day I met her my world became a much better place.

A Lesson in Self-Love

*M*y nephew, Adam and I have always had a special bond. The words that best sum up our powerful connection are honest and loving. His brother Xander is just as priceless. Adam and Xander were both in our wedding. They were so tiny but took their jobs that day so seriously. Fostering our relationships has always been one of my highest priorities, because they both mean the world to their Uncle Tom and me.

When Adam was a child, he always listened and looked deeply into my eyes whenever I spoke, absorbing everything I was saying. My words mattered to him. One day when he was twelve, he told me I was "all his own." On that visit, he also asked if he could have my antique vanity when I died. The memory makes me laugh. Either he thought I was old or loved that vanity so much, he had to lay claim to it. He is getting the vanity when I pass.

He has always been a hugger, and I always cry whenever he leaves. During one of our visits, he told me, "You will never be alone, because you will always have me." Never shy in sharing his love with me, Adam spoils me. I'm the winner in this relationship.

He graduated a year early from high school. My ZTA sorority sister, Colette, who taught him, said, "Adam is your nephew? He is the smartest student I ever had!"

Now, when I look into his eyes when we talk, I see an old soul, who possesses wisdom beyond his years. I love listening to him rhapsodize about something he loves. We often connect on things that aren't common interests of people either of our ages. We meet somewhere in the middle. We write poetry together, create crafts together and go to paint parties! We love to laugh together and just like being with each other. Adam, Xander, and I also loved taking our dog Simon to hike each time they visited. Once we were caught in a crazy rainstorm at what we dubbed "Horsky Rock Beach" and laughed hysterically.

What I loved most was taking him to see plays at the local theatre, then Broadway and then to see Panic at the Disco at Madison Square Garden. I loved my role as the fun aunt who took him on outings to New York City. I can no longer make that trip into the City, but he loves it there and goes frequently. I hope he has enough fun for both of us.

♥ ♥ ♥

The day he asked us to call him Adam we noticed he was a more realized self. I continue to ask questions to be a better aunt to Adam. I took him to New York City to give him an introduction to Stonewall, and a couple of other places to let him know that now he's part of a community where he has many historical events to honor, if he chooses to. I got him a huge pride flag. I also took him to meet and talk with other transgender youths at the LGBT Network in Bay Shore, NY. I was so impressed by Adam because he was saying who he was in such a proud and unabashed way.

Adam inspires me. He took a trip to Vienna alone this past summer. He came to visit us around Halloween. We went to see the Rocky Horror Picture Show. He helped me get into my costume as Morticia Addams in full glory. He dressed as Pugsley. We looked good if I do say so myself.

I did not have to ask him for help, he was just there…offering. When Tom dropped us off at the event, Adam came around and gave me his arm to walk me in because all I had was the cane instead of the walker. I tear up when I think of this. He was more of a gentleman than many grown men I have encountered in my lifetime.

My love for Adam, my transgender nephew, is unconditional, precious, and priceless. I hope our relationship always remains this positive. So many of us humans fight to find our self-love each day. Watching Adam show me who he was breathtaking. He is a person, who teaches me so much about myself, because I need to learn to love myself just as I am. Just as Adam does. I've learned more about self-love from him than from any self-help book I've read. It's powerful to see someone be so sure of who they are.

Adam will always be my teacher. His lesson is self-love.

81

Céline Dion, the Chosen One

S ince Céline Dion has come forth to share with the entire world about
her battle with Stiff Person Syndrome (SPS), I would like to thank
her for her grace and candor in helping open hearts and minds about this
terrible illness. I know how difficult it is to tell anyone you have a one-in-a-
million disease. In my experience, no one truly believes what you are going
through or even the name of what you are diagnosed with.

People always say, "Oh, I'm stiff, too." That insensitive response really
hurts me emotionally because my disease isn't just about that. It's about what
is happening to my entire body as a whole. Their stiffness most likely will
not kill them. Having been diagnosed with rheumatoid arthritis (RA) several
years ago, I understand the difference between stiffness from RA and from
SPS. This rare, progressive disease took my pain and stiffness to a whole new
level. SPS caused spasms so sharp and serious that I often felt like something
was about to break. Then I found out this disease really can rip tendons and
break bones. My scar tissue and even old surgery scars were getting pulled.

I remember getting charley horses that felt a little similar, but not exactly
because a charley horse never made me feel like something is going to break
or rip or bleed. The Stiff Person Syndrome spasms terrified me. They started
in my torso and my torso was getting hard. My doctor compared it to a turtle
shell trying to keep everything safe inside. I began having trouble turning
side-to-side. I was also having trouble bending over and being able to get
back up.

Before this started, I did yoga all the time, and I thought I was flexi-
ble enough. At least, I was able to get in and out of different poses without

assistance. One day I was in a pose, and I was unable to get out of it. My yoga teacher had to help me. It was almost as if I turned into a physical tree. I knew something was wrong beyond the rheumatoid arthritis or Sjogren's syndrome with which I had already been diagnosed.

Next, I started having trouble speaking, swallowing, and most obviously trouble eating. Off to the neurologist I went. Among my doctors, there was a huge concern that I had amyotrophic lateral sclerosis (ALS) better known as Lou Gehrig's disease, named after the famous New York Yankees baseball player. I began speech and swallow therapy.

I understood Céline Dion's pain, both physical and emotional, when she was telling us of her diagnosis. Watching her hold back tears was extremely powerful and moving. I knew how much she was hurting. I began to cry. I wondered how long she had been struggling.

All too well, I understand her fear of the unknown. Once this disease hits your vocal cords, larynx or pharynx area you are considered to be in the end stages. That means they can't really fix anything. Things have taken a turn for the worse at this point.

The only hope she and I have is to try to slow down the disease's progress. Mine has been picking up speed in its progress of late although I keep fighting. I hope hers is not progressing. It could go into remission for a little bit but not forever.

I never had the luxury of being in remission for any length of time. But I was determined to fight it. I started having trouble with my heart, lungs, kidneys, bladder, and brain. My brain was no longer telling my organs what to do, so dysautonomia had already set in.

You cannot imagine what it is like when you can no longer control anything.

Worse, you cannot imagine the pain when you aren't getting any support from the people who should be giving it to you. For me, this lack of compassion and support at times felt worse than the disease itself.

I feel sad that Céline Dion was the chosen one to share this disease with the world. It's rather strange to experience emotions about a famous person getting the disease. Those of us with Stiff Person Syndrome are expected to be excited because now everyone's so sure much more money will go into the research because Céline has so much money. At least doctors will pay more attention.

But the truth of the matter is, there is no happiness when somebody gets this disease, and research should be done regardless of whom has it. We shouldn't have had to wait for someone famous to get the disease in order to get the research we so desperately deserve. I constantly learn of Facebook friends in the support groups dying in their sleep. I knew this was how I was going to die.

John's Hopkins has a Stiff Person Syndrome Center but refused to take me because I had too many illnesses. Dr. Douglas Newsome instructed me to go to Mayo Clinic, because he said, "Mayo is the only hospital that can serve you properly, and most likely will be the only one that will accept you into the program."

So in late 2016 I took his advice and contacted Mayo Clinic about my situation. In April 2017 I went through a special program where the Mayo Clinic doctors had me stop all medication and diagnose me with everything all over again and then decide if I am on the right treatment plan. I came home with more diagnosis then I went with.

Originally the doctors thought that I didn't have Stiff Person Syndrome, but then the blood work came back and I did. Mayo Clinic only had the capability to check the limbs for the SPS, not the torso, which is where mine originally set in. This typically means SPS is going to attack my organs.

In January 2020, my cardiologist wanted me to go into hospice. I was all prepared and ready to go until I found out they wanted me to stop my immunoglobulin infusions. My husband and I looked at each other and the nurse and told her cancel this whole hospice thing. "I'm not going to go into hospice without seeing my neurologist first," I said. I hadn't done that yet, because the cardiologist had me so convinced that I was going to die within a month or so.

Flash forward to the present day, I started getting tons of messages about Céline having SPS and how she had to cancel her tour for 2023. I've had to cancel interviews with authors, for the same reason. We both have vocal cord dysfunction. One of my vocal cords is paralyzed, and I have edema in my larynx. I have a lot of times where I feel like I can't breathe. And doctors are telling me if my throat was so swollen, I wouldn't be able to talk at all. That same day I saw my speech and swallow therapist, and he said, "Oh no, you have edema in your throat. We have all seen it." It's the worst feeling in the world when you have to give up something you love so, so much. I love interviewing authors and doing my shows as much as I love air. I can only imagine that Céline Dion's sense of loss had to be so much bigger than mine. She was giving up a spot on the world's stage. But to be honest, I couldn't comprehend that level of loss because mine felt so immense.

It is with both dignity and grace that I decided to share my journey with each of you. It is because of your love and prayers that I am always fighting! I am so grateful. I'm now 53 years old and have had several autoimmune diseases since age 18. The doctors are saying I am in the end stages of my life. I have come to terms with that. Catholic Home Care helped me prepare. My body will be going to the Molecular & Cell Biology Lab at NYU Downstate. All Tom has to do is dial a 1-800 number once I pass away and the lab will have a funeral director pick up my body and take me directly to the University.

Knowing that I carried these diseases for a reason gives some comfort. Hopefully I can help even just one person. Maybe a lot of people.

Once they are done studying me (under five years) they cremate what's left of my body, and then they will bury my ashes in New Jersey at a beautiful cemetery where people can visit me if they choose. I had other choices like being sent in an urn back to Tom or another family member or to be buried at sea. I chose the cemetery so people could visit if they wanted and not to interfere with Tom's life. Hopefully he finds new love by then. I learned from a book by Emily Belden called "Husband Material," that I definitely do not want to be sent home to him.That can cause major trouble, just read her book. It's so entertaining.

Doctors believe that many of these autoimmune diseases may have been been the repercussions of a cervical fracture (C-7) I suffered during college from a car accident. The doctors at Mayo Clinic said that spinal fluid got into my bloodstream and caused an infection that was never treated when I fractured my neck. There's also the possibility that all of the trauma I've endured in my life has contributed to the state of my health as well. I would agree because with each trauma I could actually feel things changing within my body. It was a visceral response. Most especially Jennifer's death and my hysterectomy.

Altogether different, I'd been born with common variable immunodeficiency. I had endometriosis, Hashimoto's disease, RA, Sjogrens. Then, in 2017 I was diagnosed with Stiff Person Syndrome, a rare acquired neurological disorder. This led to chronic inflammatory demyelinating polyneuropathy (CIDP) and autonomic dysfunction throughout my body. In July 2020 we discovered the SPS entered my heart. I now have Lasix resistant congestive heart failure (CHF) because my brain isn't sending the correct signals to my heart.

I have been hospitalized countless times with the average stay being eleven days. We tried to come up with a plan. We are still looking for one. Everything is incorrectly communicating. I have lymphedema from all of the water I carry. It's so uncomfortable and quite embarrassing if I'm being honest.

The congestive heart failure I have is not typical. It isn't functional; it is electrical. My brain can send a signal to stop it at any time. My only fear is my hearing everyone's voice at least one time should this happen. I will not take my life for granted. I will not take my loved one's lives for granted. I am trying to FaceTime with everybody when we speak.

My memoir, "Annie's Song: Dandelions, Dreams and Dogs" is a group of essays and poems. Most were written during a grief writing class I take on Sundays with Diane Zinna. Echo Garrett and Connor Garrett of Lucid House Publishing are my publishers.

I go to bed each night with the "Now I lay me down to sleep" prayer hoping for all the time to accomplish all I'd like to accomplish: speaking with all the people I'd like to speak with; writing all I'd like to write; and loving all of whom I would love to love like my husband and babies. I'd especially love to see my nephews and niece get married.

But I've had a fabulous life. I have love so many never know. I am truly blessed. I am fine imagining going to heaven. I trust I'll be happy there, too.

Thank you to all of my best friends, who are there for me every single day.

This is the best information online for Stiff Person Syndrome also known as Tin Man Disease: http://www.thetinman.org/progressionandstages.html.

My Irish Heart Lives On

Oh! Éire!
To see you again as the plane lands in Dublin and put my feet on your
land once more would be the pulse of my very lifeblood and pride.
To smell your air again in the city near the Ha-penny Bridge or the
Post Office,
To breathe you in at the waters of Donabate as my heart turns into
a shamrock,
I become one with you again in memory.
To hug my cousins, share Sláintes and songs at the pub, dance the Irish
jigs and reels into the night, banging my memories into the floors, with
the prayer that my soul lives on in the nicks I leave on the wooden floor.

Oh! Éire!
To hear your accent and laughter again is what I just blew today's dande-
lion wishes on.
These wishes won't come true, but for tonight I'll watch you on the
screen in my living room.
I'll smile for my memories of you are immense.

Oh! Éire!
I hope this dream comes true for another little girl like I once was.
I was so very lucky to know Ireland's breeze.
That little girl, Ann-Bridget, with the face full of freckles and the
dreams as big as my green eyes,
with Ireland reflecting in them like a pond at dawn,
will weep tears that can't be wiped away.
for all I did from the moment I was first getting off the plane from
America will whisper in my ears for years.

Oh! Éire!
Dandelions and Queen Anne's Lace will follow me like the nettles that
stung me in the fields I ran through with a boy I once loved.
Memories that would sting and itch like part of me

screaming to never leave or forget.
That bittersweet pain that was once so satisfied would never feel that
Gaelic breathe of air again
or that first imagined kiss from the Irish boy.

Oh! Éire!
That little girl inside me is screaming and bleeding to get out and on the
next plane,
to be stung by nettles again, and again,
until I go back in time.

Yet, I can't let her go.
That little girl inside me and I must sit here together and just watch the
pictures and movies and music and dancing on the television.
I will hold her hand,
And we will tell each other we are not alone.

Irish hearts always live on.
Like the whispers on the wind of a girl's first love.

Dandelion seeds!
Please go and find Éire's next soulmate
and welcome her home!

May you be her first true love, too!

Go share stories of love and pride with her, so that she, too, can know
the love I still carry in my heart.

It has been such a gift.

Irish hearts live on,
Because we never leave home.

I don't need to visit again.

Éire lives in me.
Those nettle stings made sure of it.
I have already said my goodbyes.
Gratefully, Ireland's earth became one with me.

McHorsky's 38th Annual Grief Tour

*A*nnouncing McHorsky's 38th Annual Grief World Tour of the "Heart Healing BandI'!" Celebrating Life Each Year Since 1984!

All concerts take place right here on Long Island since the lead singer can't travel. So, they play at Jones Beach theatre during the theatre open season, and at the Paramount Theatre in Huntington, during the colder months.

The concert is always opens with One Love Dog Rescue volunteers singing "Who Let the Dogs Out!" (they'll have dogs available for adoption and accept donations.)

Then, the Ladies of the Zeta Tau Alpha Sorority will sing "We are Family!"

The 2022 concert series began on April 5th to honor the loss of her stepmother who sang lots of songs about strong women. The love between a mother and daughters is celebrated.

If you miss it this year, make sure you get your tickets for next year, it's something you don't want to miss because McHorsky's stepmother was all about love. While being without her is difficult, the band works hard to share her message of love and her celebration of life.

The band played live at the theater as McHorsky was zoomed in via video from her hospital bed for her opening song "Unstoppable"! The crowd was still going wild.

Then, they all come out and sang "I've Got Friends in High Places." (Yes, they changed a word)

McHorsky sings the finale song "I'm Alive" with her "Top Notch Friends," singers Erica, Noelle, Susan, Val, Crystal, Serena, Echo, Meryl, and Patricia. Then the group was all there to sing all the other songs. The groupies loved them, too because they are always with her...supporting her!! These are her constant friends.

Canceling is never an option! Mistakes can be made and forgiveness is offered.

Everyone that attended the concert was given a free band t-shirt with their zebra with the breast cancer pink ribbon and shamrock logo. The zebra represents the rare diseases that McHorsky is fighting, the breast cancer that she lost her stepmother to, and the shamrock that represents her livelihood and reminds her of her best friend Jennifer whom she lost to murder at just 15. That's why these concerts have been held since 1984.

While McHorsky was not officially in attendance, the concert was a huge hit! You could feel the camaraderie and love!

There was Italian and Irish food available at the venue, as well as cardiac diet foods. And if you were a vegetarian, you were sure to find something you could feast on.

Compression socks, braces, walkers, and anything to help with your daily needs were there. There were plenty of books for the sick and their caregivers.

Every two years we ask our fans to sign a petition to keep the person that murdered Jennifer in prison.

Each month there is a reason to grieve, so there is a concert and a cause.

Each concert seats 223 and 410 gets free tickets to the next concert since those are the hospital rooms McHorsky seems to always in. We will add seats as necessary.

This is a fabulous event for the entire family! Come join us! Call the theatre for tickets!

$\mathcal{84}$

Céline Dion and Me

$\mathcal{I}$ was so sorry to learn that Céline Dion suffers from Stiff Person Syndrome. I cannot imagine not being able to sing and be Céline. Her money or fame won't make her disease any easier to handle. Stiff Person Syndrome does not discriminate. I would not wish this even on my worst enemy.

I had to stop interviewing authors on an almost a daily basis for the same reasons Céline announced that she could no longer sing. This disease is attacking my larynx, esophagus, vocal cords and more in that area. One of my vocal cords has stiffened. I have severe arytenoid/interarytenoid edema erythema. Vocal Cord Dysfunction was diagnosed along with moderately severe pharngeal-esophageal dysphagia. I need swallow, voice, and respiratory therapy. I lose my voice if I talk too much, or it gets hoarse. The spasms, sudden apnea, my oxygen levels, or blood pressure dropping too quickly could cause death. My heart issues put me in the hospital quite often.

I am at a point where I am trying desperately not to go back to the hospital. From being in the Stiff Person Syndrome support group on Facebook, I understand that most of us die in our sleep. I have accepted this. I am even prepared. I am also in the ALS (amyotrophic lateral sclerosis) support group out of New York City. I was referred by my occupational therapist since there isn't an in-person Stiff Person Syndrome support group. I was told the end stages are the same for both diseases, so the leader of the group, who is a doctor, accepted me.

I have trouble breathing when I walk a few steps and it often turns into a hypertensive crisis. My left side is numb, head to toe. I fall. I can even fall out of my seat. My kidneys have gone into acute kidney failure, but we fixed that. My heart is all confused and my bladder is ridiculous. I need a bladder pacemaker, but I cannot get one due to the possibility of infection. I developed cellulitis because I couldn't recover from two tiny holes put into my sacrum for the "tens wires." These two tiny holes wreaked havoc on my body for almost two months. From now on only lifesaving or necessary surgeries for me. I was told my body is too unwell to heal and too tired for another contraption in it.

My eyes have trouble staying open and the left side of my face droops sometimes. My chest feels like it is getting crushed most of the time. My ADL (activities of daily living) are all compromised. Everything is difficult. My ribs feel bruised and swollen. Sometimes simply breathing hurts. I have recently started just falling asleep suddenly and waking up very confused. I am being tested to find out the reason for this latest development.

I rarely discuss the six-disc herniations, one bulge, central canal stenosis in spine/neck, or osteoporosis and rheumatoid arthritis in various joints because the pain from this constellation of problems isn't as bad as the Stiff Person Syndrome's spasms and stiffness. All the water weight the disease has caused is extremely painful. I have lymphedema. I have dysautonomia, which is another beast of its own. My body cannot regulate itself at all.

"You will know them by their love" is a quote I admire, because it is so true. "Born to Shimmer, Born to Shine" is another, because I'm determined to SHIMMER AND SHINE each day. If you are a person who helps me with this goal, I thank you.

My primary care physician, Dr. Brian Pultz of Bethpage, NY, would always say, "We haven't found your monster yet!" He and I were convinced there was an answer and cure to all of this madness I go through each day or at least a better treatment option. One day, he said, "Annie, I'm not keeping you well. I keep getting you well. I feel like I'm changing your illnesses. I am not going a good enough job for you. I think you have an immunodeficiency."

He referred me to Dr. Lisa Katz Buglino, an immunologist, who put me through a battery of tests and studied my history. She said, "You have common variable immunodeficiency." I was relieved to get that diagnosis, and she started me on IVIG infusions.

Dr. Pultz also told me he read about Dr. Yao (rheumatologist at Stony Brook University and Cleveland Clinic) and believe I may have Yao syndrome, a disease he defined. He is a professor in Stony Brook's Department of Medicine and Chief of Rheumatology, Allergy, and Immunology. He is studying autoinflammatory diseases and is director of The Center for Autoinflammatory Diseases. Dr. Pultz suggested if I didn't have Yao syndrome, at least Dr. Yao had the knowledge and authority to find a disease if I had one, even if it was new and had to be named. He said he wouldn't be surprised if one was named after me.

I have immunodeficiency, autoimmune, and autoinflammatory diseases. It is so surprising the number of people who don't know the difference between the three of these. Being immunocompromised is not the same as having immunodeficiency. When your body is fighting all three it is a battle. It is exhausting battling them, but also trying to get people to understand.

I have also been diagnosed with chronic inflammatory demyelinating polyneuropathy, common variable immunodeficiency, Sluder neuralgia, rheumatoid arthritis, Sjogren's syndrome, hypersomnia, sinus tachycardia, high blood pressure, heart disease, hypoxemia, along with a bunch of other secondary things. When you put these all together it is different than having one or two alone, even the doctors get stumped.

I got a second opinion with a neurological specialist at a large medical center. After looking over all my records he determined that Dr. Gudesblatt missed Bechet's syndrome and that I needed Rituxan infusions. Dr. Gudesblatt agreed with him. There is a significant possibility I have amyloids, and he said that it would most likely be genetic amyloidosis. I've noticed most doctors have stopped testing me for things and are just trying to treat my symptoms.

I called to make an appointment with Dr. Yao, which we thought would be months later, but I answered a few questions over the phone, and I was given an appointment within three weeks.

Off to the specialist I went. Dr. Yao did genetic testing on me. He believed I had Yao syndrome just by looking at me. He tested for a few genes besides the Yao syndrome. The results came back, and I have the Yao syndrome gene mutation, and another one that could encompass the rheumatoid arthritis, Stiff Person Syndrome, and a lot of the various diseases I've already been diagnosed with. This gene has been proven to cause issues in each system in the body. It is known as the NLRP-12 gene and is considered ultra-rare.

I have the best medical team. We are now adding an additional infusion called Rituxan to which I am highly allergic. But, I need it so badly that the chance of anaphylaxis is worth what this drug can help me with. So, Benadryl will be on board, and my friend, Vicki, knows to watch me like a hawk. I know the nurses will, but having Vicki there makes me less scared. It should not only help the Stiff Person Syndrome but also the rheumatoid arthritis, Sjogrens, Yao, and NLRP-12 syndromes.

I've spent most of my life trying to live above the noise of my body's insidious cry as it was being attacked, cell by cell removing nerve fibers and more. I knew something had to be systemically wrong. I've lost all of my reflexes.

I was already told I had a few rare diseases, two of which only one in a million people have. I recently learned I carry a gene called "ultra-rare." I was the 28th person diagnosed with it in the entire world, the third in the U.S.A. There are now more than 100 people diagnosed with it. Researchers discovered that it was connected to pregnant woman in Ireland during the Great Famine and other countries with famines. The DNA of women who were pregnant during this time changed to feed their fetuses and created the NLRP-12 gene. Apparently, this gene mutated due to severe adversity. I've fallen so far down this rabbit hole with researching online, especially on pubmed.gov. I want to learn as much as I can. Researchers say there are a lot of people with this disease who just don't know they have it yet. The reason they have no clue is simply because they have not gotten sick enough yet to be sent to someone like Dr. Yao for gene testing. So, the gene may not be as rare as initially believed.

I have spent so much time in my life being called a liar or losing people I love because they couldn't deal with my illnesses, or my sheer grief from feeling so unwell and losing the ability to do things. I have been called a pin cushion when I knew there was an answer, and I wasn't going to give up until I found it. I could feel that I was dying. I was going to keep being tested for things, because there was an answer, and I want to be around for years to come. I was in agony from head-to-toe, but I was dysfunctional for a reason. I could sense the decline in my health.

Once we found out about the ultra-rare gene mutation, I had hope for a treatment. I learned perseverance when I had endometriosis for five years and not one person believed me. I was treated with meds as a hypochondriac, only to learn I did have endometriosis. But the doctors caught it so late I needed a full hysterectomy at only age 23. Many people don't understand the pain and scars I carry, and how I will never get over my miscarriages and not being a mother because of doctors not listening to me. I decided back then that would never happen again. I would always stand up for myself medically. I had to advocate for myself and made it my mission to educate others about becoming their own advocate.

My speech/swallow doctor, Dr. Amato, told me that I impress him each day. He is always learning about other parts of me not working or spasms so strong that they can cause bones to break. The pain is excruciating. When Dr. Amato heard about the stroke and TIAs he was shocked. He says I owe my life to keeping up with my therapy and my positive attitude. He knew I invented something for me to do so I don't become a wallflower, so trust me while some authors might get frustrated that I cancel, move dates, or ask for help with interviews, it is genuine. It was always up to them if they want to tell the world I ask for too much, or you want to help me. Sometimes you need to wait for me to feel better, but I always remember the authors who were kind to me. I try to give back as much as I get from people.

This time I'm fighting because I am not accepting that this is it. I'm not accepting that my life is going to be over soon or that I will not be able to get off this couch anymore. I want my freedom back, or at least a little bit more of it. Using the walker, not being able to stand for more than two to five minutes without shaking like crazy or falling or caring for myself properly is overwhelming. It is difficult to have guests or for me to go anywhere.

I have noticed these diseases are harder in the dark months. My advice, if you have even one of these, is find a hobby. I'm a book reviewer, and I love it. I also color, meditate, research ancestry, and listen to grounding music in the background all day. I light candles and pray. I have FaceTime visits with friends each day, I call it "Coffeetime" when it is with my BFF, Susan. I often find a new craft. I do chair exercise or chair dance. This is all in addition to my swallow and speech therapy. I also have plenty of puzzle books, which I need to do to exercise my brain.

Try to follow the cardiac or Mediterranean diet. Those help both physically and mentally.

I can't take walks, but I do things for 10 minutes each hour. Join an exchange program, so you are sending and getting mail. It could be postcards to packages. I love getting mail. I find the more I'm involved in life, the more I'm living, even if it looks different than my old life. I must learn to find joy in the new normal.

I remember being in pain and unable to do physical activity most of my life. I even forged a letter to my gym teacher in high school so that I wouldn't have to use the rings because my arms, especially wrist and elbows, were hurting so badly and I was so weak. I shattered my elbow when I was five, so I thought that was the reason. At the time, it never dawned on me that would cause only my right arm to be weak, not both.

Recent biopsy results showed a rare and chronic case of an infection called actinomycosis in my throat. From my records, it appears this could be

in my central nervous system, bones, and the reason my nose cartilage col-
lapsed, and why my sinuses and ears are not well so often.

This is most likely why my face droops, I have slurred speech, or I have
trouble swallowing and even speaking sometimes. I choke on food, drinks,
and even my own saliva sometimes.

Dr. Pultz has helped me discover so much about my body. He said every
test I take is going to come back with a problem, so we try not to do too many
tests at this point.

He recently said, "There's a long road ahead." I am determined to have
a long life, even though I am prepared should it go the other way. I am prepared to die, thanks to Catholic Home Care helping me when I was going
into hospice. Words cannot describe how grateful I am for all the love and
support I get. My friends help me more than you know. I trust this has everything to do with my still being here.

Dr. Gudesblatt always says, "Stop counting these diseases. You have systemic
neurological autoimmune syndrome and common variable Immunodeficiency."

No matter what I have on the list of diseases, Stiff Person Syndrome is the
biggest culprit. I am at the end stages of this disease. I could stop treatment if
I want. I choose not to. They say it's end stage because of what the Stiff Person
Syndrome is affecting.

I keep looking for a new answer, but I am constantly told to accept this.
Everything is always called "disease progression." I am accepting that comfort is key. Between my psychiatrist, Dr. Donoghue, and counselor, Eman
Said, I am held together. I count on them for so much, and they are both
amazing. They are both critically important to my care and make themselves
available whenever I need them. The best advice I can offer is to get yourself a
Joanie. She is my physical therapist, and she really cares about me. She wants
me to improve or at least plateau for as long as I can. She believes in me so
much that I believe in myself. Stiff Person Syndrome will flair from stress

and causes depression, agoraphobia, and more. I thank God for my medical team and the people in my life who support me.

♥ ♥ ♥

I'm trying to educate myself with what's happening to me, so people are clear as to my condition. Some say it's asking for pity, which is so naive. If you have a rare disease, it is your job to help teach others who may have the same issues. I would hope that I can share that even through troubles with these diseases, I can still have a bright and happy life. That is my biggest wish.

I am an open book. Because I want to be an advocate to help teach doctors and nurses and patients about this one-in-a-million disease and the other rare diseases I have. I do not write about any of it for you to ever feel sorry for me.

Annie's Song is my love letter to you. Music is included so you can hear my story this way, too. I don't want anyone to just read this book, I hope people experience it. My hope is that people learn empathy and compassion for people going through things like I am. But most of all, I hope you feel the love as you read it.

Read more on Stiff Person Syndrome at

https://stiffperson.org

and

http://www.thetinman.org/progressionandstages.html

Dandelion Dreams

"**Y**our respiratory and throat muscles have become too weak to sustain you for much longer because they are going to get weaker with each day that passes," said Dr. Gudesblatt, my neurologist.

All I could say was, "Okay, thank you." I knew what was happening to my body. I could feel it. He did not need to tell me. People couldn't see it, but I was shutting down. It wasn't just my throat.

"Are you sure you understand what I'm telling you?" asked Dr. G.

"Yes, I'll be fine," was all I had to say.

"Ok, Annie, but I'm going to call you tomorrow to make sure we're on the same page. I'm not comfortable that you understand the magnitude of this."

I shuffle out of Dr. G's office, pushing my walker. Each leg is so very heavy and harder to move than usual. Maybe it's the knowledge that I'm moving one step closer towards my permanent slumber with each step. His confirmation was intensely profound.

I remember getting home from that appointment, laying down on the couch and snuggling with my pup, Sullivan and falling fast asleep. I might have been dreaming before my eyes closed. My lids felt heavy and soon I was in a deep sleep, which is typical for someone with hypersomnia.

I remember what I dreamed so clearly.

With each step I took I started floating up and up, higher into the sky. I felt light. The thousand pounds of deadweight I was carrying like luggage I could never unpack was falling off me. When everything holding me down was gone, I realized I was floating in the wind and sitting on a dandelion seed that a child had just wished upon. Only I believed this time my wish that was going to true, too.

I sat on that little seed from a yellow flower that most people consider a weed and felt true happiness. To me this seed had beauty in life because could nourish and feed people. These flowers made beautiful bouquets that children would pick for their mothers on Mother's Day or on a random Sunday to say: "I love you."

In death and also transformed like me, there were others who also blew wishes on the dandelions and were floating on pillows of soft white individually packed lacey wishes. They formed a vast silvery cloud of what so many of us need: a magical promise of hope.

I view my life similarly. Let me explain.

I was so comfortable and felt I was right where I needed to be. I was becoming one with the breeze in the sky and the sunshine. We were able to sway in the wind as we crossed towns and countries, visiting each of our friends and family. I even visited some of my no longer friends.

Why visit my no longer friends? You see, they may have stopped loving me, but I never stopped loving them. I left each of them a whisper of love. My friends who were still loving me were also left a love note along with a note of solace for when I'm gone. I wanted them to know my soul was flying free and that I was intensely relieved. There would be nothing for anyone to be sad about. No tears for me. Just smiles. Only love should exist for me once I'm gone.

New York University Downstate Medical Center has come to pick up my broken body and make good use of it. My body didn't serve me as well as it could, but it will serve a purpose for others. This weighed down, non-working stiff never gave me a child. My painful and sick from head-to-toe body is no longer the shell of my soul's existence. I no longer have to carry its many burdens—let alone the burdens some say I put upon them with my illnesses.

No more cries for my soul to get out. No more screaming silently so I don't upset people.

I now exist only here on the dandelion seed, floating like a breath of fresh air until I make it to heaven safe in the knowledge I will be at home once again with those loved ones and pets who passed before me.

They've been waiting. I've heard them whisper in my ear long before I died. There is a party being planned in heaven where I'll be able to dance. I'll be able to hold my drink without fear of dropping it. I'll be able to eat without a care in the world about choking. I can walk my dog, Simon. I won't need a week of recovery from being out just a few hours.

I know I'll see each of you again in heaven, too. I stayed here on earth as long as I could. I promise I fought. I am free. I feel you will have a huge sense of freedom without me, too. I know being part of my life isn't easy. I have always acknowledged my blessings for everyone who continued loving me.

I believe I was beautiful and so was my life. My life had a purpose even if it was only found in death. Just ask that child being healed by the lifesaving medicine able to be created because of the cells studied from my body's shell. I believe the study of my body will help further medicine. NYU Downstate believes it, too. They are taking my body even though it is overweight. All of the rare diseases are too valuable not to study.

If you see a dandelion that's gone to seed, pick it, make a wish, and blow gently. Someone's soul may be trying to get to heaven, or it may be me wanting to say hello to you. Either way, simply remember me and smile.

♥ ♥ ♥

Tom is rubbing my shoulders to wake me, telling me I've been talking in my sleep about wishes and parties and beautiful this and that. He asks if I am okay. I reply, "I was just absorbing all Dr. Gudesblatt just told me today"

I'm slowly waking up. I have often since had this dream of the dandelion seed. I believe I will travel to heaven on a seed from a dandelion weed a child has just wished upon. But it will be my wish of rest finally coming true. I am so tired. Each day more tired than the day before.

ACKNOWLEDGMENTS

Above all, to my caring, loving, and supportive husband, Tom: my deepest gratitude for his hard work to care for me and our family. Especially watching our fur babies when I was taking writing classes.

To our dogs Simon, Sullivan, Bonnie and Daphne, and our cats Bella, Mikah, Petra, Zero and Luna: You all light up my life.

Laurel, Simon's other mom. Thank you for trusting us with him.

Thank you to my brother Kenneth Horsky and his family. Love to Yvonne Guenther, Sondra Thomson, Xander, and Adam Horsky for always believing in me. For my nephews for asking if one of them needed to live with me, since I had no kids and they wanted me to be happy and I'd make the best mom. Their hearts are so full of love.

Thanks to my in-laws, Mr. and Mrs. McDonnell, as well as Erica Firkin for always going the extra mile helping care for me.

Thank you to Serena for all she does for me from the book club to loving me.

Special thanks to Mandy Haynes for helping me realize that I do deserve for my dreams to come true and for encouraging me to keep going.

I cannot express enough thanks to my teacher, Diane Zinna and my classmates for their continued witnessing of my life's journey.

To Connor, Kevin, and Echo Garrett for believing in my work. This book only exists because of them. Echo spent relentless hours listening to my work.

I offer my sincere appreciation for the learning opportunities provided to me by The Muse Writing Center in Norfolk, VA.

The completion of this book could not have been accomplished without the support of my friends. They led me to find the strength to open up and share these stories. My ZTA sorority sisters for always lifting me up. My college friends. My friends from Darryl's, Sam's Club, the apartment complexes in Virginia and Access IT. Friends from my shaman tribe, especially Doris and Joel Diamond. My One Love Dog Rescue family. Friends from the book world. My doctors, nurses, medical team, and the best physical therapist, Joanie, for helping me navigate my life in a positive light.

Extra gratitude to my second-grade best friend/blood sister, Stephanie, and BFF Susan and godson Grant.

I am grateful for the support of Ann-Marie Nieves, Patricia Sands, Meg Nocero, Leslie Rasmussen, Suzanne Simonetti, Alison Ragsdale, and Meryl Ain for always cheering me on and making me believe I could do anything.

To Serena, Phyllis, Vicki, Erica, Nancy and Noelle for always listening to my writing. To Crystal and Val for loving me unconditionally. You are all the best girlfriends. Vince Spinnato, "I know what you did last summer!"

Extra thanks to readers, book reviewers, bloggers, book clubs, book shops, podcasters, and everyone supporting authors.

I would be remiss if I didn't thank my elementary school teacher, Mr. Book, for making me believe I could be whoever I wanted to be, while introducing me to books and writing book reviews for the school newspaper.

And, my mom in Heaven. I'll always thank you for my sentimental journeys. You understood me and loved me unconditionally.

And still, after all this time,
The sun never says to the earth,
"You owe Me."

Look what happens with
A love like that,
It lights the Whole Sky.

-Hafiz

ABOUT THE AUTHOR

A lifelong reader and advocate for writers and books, Annie McDonnell is an alumnus of High Point University, North Carolina, class of 1991. In 2006, she entered a contest with *Elle* and became a book reviewer for the magazine. When *Elle* stopped running book reviews in print, Annie moved to blogging and eventually began *The Write Review*. An entire community was born. Her previously published work includes a poem and essay in an anthology called *Once Upon Another Time*.

In December 2020, she was the recipient of the Doug Marlette Award for lifetime achievement in Book Promotion. In February 2021, the Annie McDonnell Book Award was announced, honoring her dedication to the literary community and her courage and strength in battling a rare illness called Stiff Person Syndrome. Annie writes book reviews, articles, endorsements for authors; conducts author interviews; and consults with authors on promotions and events. In addition, she administers the *World of the Write Review*. Proceeds from *Annie's Song* will go to One Love Dog Rescue, The Muse Writing Center, the Pat Conroy Literary Center, and the Stiff Person Syndrome Research Foundation. She also volunteers for One Love Dog Rescue and supports both adult and children's literacy. Annie lives in Mastic, New York, with her husband Tom, three beautiful dogs, and five lovely cats.

CPSIA information can be obtained
at www.ICGtesting.com
Printed in the USA
JSHW011924180723
45004JS00004B/97

9 781950 495351